Counter-Narrative

For Sandra

Counter-Narrative

*How Progressive Academics
Can Challenge Extremists
and Promote Social Justice*

H. L. Goodall, Jr.

Left
Coast
Press
Inc.

Walnut Creek
California

2010

green press
INITIATIVE

Left Coast Press is committed to preserving ancient forests and natural resources. We elected to print this title on 30% post consumer recycled paper, processed chlorine free. As a result, for this printing, we have saved:

2 Trees (40' tall and 6-8" diameter)
1 Million BTUs of Total Energy
144 Pounds of Greenhouse Gases
693 Gallons of Wastewater
42 Pounds of Solid Waste

Left Coast Press made this paper choice because our printer, Thomson-Shore, Inc., is a member of Green Press Initiative, a nonprofit program dedicated to supporting authors, publishers, and suppliers in their efforts to reduce their use of fiber obtained from endangered forests.

For more information, visit www.greenpressinitiative.org

Environmental impact estimates were made using the Environmental Defense Paper Calculator. For more information visit: www.papercalculator.org.

Left Coast Press
Inc.

LEFT COAST PRESS, INC.
1630 North Main Street, #400
Walnut Creek, CA 94596
http://www.LCoastPress.com

ISBN 978-1-59874-562-7 hardcover
ISBN 978-1-59874-563-4 paperback

Library of Congress Cataloging-in-Publication Data
Goodall, H. Lloyd.
   Counter-narrative : how progressive academics can challenge extremists and promote social justice / H.L. Goodall, Jr.
      p. cm.
   Includes bibliographical references.
   ISBN 978-1-59874-562-7 (hbk. : alk. paper)–ISBN 978-1-59874-563-4 (pbk. : alk. paper)
1. Radicalism–United States. 2. Conservatism–United States. 3. Social justice–United States. 4. Communication in politics–United States. 5. Mass media and public opinion–United States. 6. United States–Politics and government–2009- 7. United States–Social policy–21st century. I. Title.
   HN90.R3G64 2010
   306.20973'09051–dc22
                        2010031881

Printed in the United States of America

∞™ The paper used in this publication meets the minimum requirements of American National Standard for Information Sciences—Permanence of Paper for Printed Library Materials, ANSI/NISO Z39.48–1992.

Contents

Do I dare / Disturb the universe?

~ T. S. Eliot

America will never be destroyed
from the outside.
If we falter and lose our freedoms,
it will be because we destroyed ourselves.

~ Abraham Lincoln

When you are right you cannot be too radical;
when you are wrong, you cannot be too conservative.

~ Martin Luther King, Jr.

The trouble is that once you see it,
you can't unsee it.
And once you've seen it, keeping quiet,
saying nothing
becomes as political an act
as speaking out.
There's no innocence.
Either way, you're accountable.

~ Arundhati Roy

Preface

This book began in an email with Mitch Allen, my publisher and friend, as a way to amuse him while he suffered the often joyless burden of American citizenship known as "jury duty." A joyless burden only because instead of being offered a chance to serve, we end up wasting a day or two before being summarily dismissed or disqualified. In America, it seems, the last thing most attorneys want is an intelligent jury. Particularly if one of those jury members is a professor of communication or if another one owns a publishing house. Denied our Constitutional right to serve, we have largely become cynical about the jury selection process. It is sad, but so very true. Hence, our email exchange.

Mitch and I share a progressive view of America. We also share a love of words, stories, and an appreciation for the power of narratives to shape not only ideas and selves, but also nations and destinies. Because of our progressive view and our understanding of the power of stories, we share a concern that the narrative told by the radical extremist fringe on the far, far right of the American political landscape is gaining traction with at least a few conservatives and more than a few independents. One result is that American politics, always loud, contested and full of passion, has become toxic.

I have been struck during the past year, the year following the election of Barack Obama, by the change in tone, style, and tactics used by the radical extremist right to attack any idea proposed by

Democrats or moderate Republicans. I have also been strangely captivated by an emerging narrative evoked or represented by pundits, writers, politicians, and activists on the right. It is a singularly unified narrative that projects a nation in chaos, marked by disorder and Godlessness; a Black president who was not born in America and who may be a Muslim; challenges to individual human rights and existing laws drawn from literal readings of the Constitution as well as fictional representations of the views of the founding fathers; a general call to arms to "take back the country," reinstate something akin to a Reagan Caliphate, and throw out the Crusaders from the center and left who have invaded the political and social landscape, seized Congress and the presidency, and threaten "progress" that is a cleverly disguised socialism associated with much needed health care and financial system reform.

I notice this core narrative and its ideological construction because for the past year I have been part of a Department of Defense interdisciplinary research team charged with studying extremist narratives in the Islamic world. I cannot help but see a frightening commonality between the world projected by Osama bin Laden and the world projected by Glenn Beck, Sarah Palin, Rush Limbaugh, Michele Bachmann, Michael Savage, and others on the far right in American politics. Theirs is an extremist narrative and an extremist worldview.

For those readers unfamiliar with the foundational radical extremist Islamic narrative, here's the short version: Our world is in chaos and disorder and we have turned away from True Islam. Only by reinstating the Caliphate and with it, Sharia law, can Allah's will be done and order restored. To do this means engaging in a holy *jihad* against the Crusaders who have invaded our land and taken over our governments, and whose Western ways threaten our beliefs and values. These Crusaders are enabled by apostate regimes, and those regimes, too, must be opposed. For it is the duty of all righteous Muslims to rise up and defend our faith and our lands from enemies near and far. They say they want peace and stability, but we know that is not true. They have brought war and instability instead.

As a result of seeing this pronounced similarity between American and Islamist extremist narratives, I have also been paying more attention than I used to pay to news broadcasts and Internet sites and following political activities on the right—marches, pro-tests, rallies, conventions, attempts to disrupt public meetings, attempts to shout down the president, and so on—with an eye to understanding the broader purpose and goals of these actions. In particular, I want to more fully understand the rhetorical relation-ships between their radical extremist narrative and resulting radical extremist actions.

Three caveats. First, I am speaking throughout this book of a radi-cal political movement comprised of members drawn from a wide spectrum of right wing groups—from Teabaggers and militias to Keep America Safers to mainstream conservatives, from disaffected independents to thoroughly connected and well-financed pundits, comedians, news readers, and spokespersons. While these groups and individuals are different, they tend to share a similar core nar-rative. And because they share and often repeat the storylines and soundbites from a similar core narrative, it would be easy to per-ceive that they also share the same political views and ideological vision for the country. This is not necessarily true.

While I celebrate the messiness of our democratic political sys-tem and welcome debates with conservatives and independents alike, the groups that I am targeting in this book are those on the *fringes* of the radical extremist right. Or at least they are on the fringes as of this writing. Which is to say, I am targeting a relatively small population of individuals—some familiar enough in our medi-ated culture and others who are never seen—who are, in my humble opinion, posing real threats to both our political system and to the American way of life. They are politically and narratively, if you will, an American Taliban. They have in essence declared a holy war on everyone who disagrees with their views, and they use a propaganda campaign based on fear to spread their extremist ideology. My fear and the reason for this book is that spread of ideology. Just as al Qaeda is less an effective political organization than it is a highly successful ideology, so too is the extremist narrative of the American right becoming a highly successful ideology. Like a virus, it spreads; like an aggressive form of cancer, it grows rapidly.

So my first caveat is this one: *I am not talking about most Americans on the right.* I am talking about a small minority of fanatics. My fear is the conservative and independent appropriation of the radicals' extremist rhetoric in the service of spreading that narrative, as well as the lack of conservative outcry against the tactics of disrupting civil discourse, as it seems to have done with the Hutaree militia (see chapter 6), will lead others to embrace the ideology and to act on it.[1]

I live in Arizona. I have witnessed first-hand what happens when the fringe relocates its anger, its fear, its money, and its rhetoric from radio and television listening outposts to seats of power in the state legislature. As I wrote this book in the spring of 2010, my state passed new laws requiring candidates to produce birth certificates to prove they are American; it passed a bill allowing anyone to carry guns without permits into bars and anywhere else that doesn't strictly forbid it; and it encouraged police to detain anyone who looked "reasonably suspicious" and required them to produce identity "papers." Fortunately, on July 28, 2010, the last of these bills was blocked by federal judge Susan Bolton, but the political struggle it represents is far from settled. Furthermore, its appeal has spread to other state legislatures.

As a concerned citizen I have watched, with increasing incredulity, as that same state legislature, seizing the opportunity created by our near economic collapse to apply far-right ideology to the problem, closed state parks and rest areas; sold the state Capitol, prisons, and other buildings; and reduced the budget of my university by over two hundred million dollars while requiring us to admit more students. As Pulitzer-prize winning author Timothy Egan, piggybacking on Jon Stewart's observation that "Arizona is the meth lab of democracy," put it: "Arizona is more than a laboratory for intemperate times: this place is a warning of what a state can look like when it's run by talk-radio demagogues and their television cohorts."[2]

It's not only liberals who rail against the far-right wing, media-inspired madness, or what conservative blogger Julian Sanchez calls "epistemic closure."[3] Referring to the power of conservative outlets such as Fox News and *National Review,* as well as to talk-show stars Rush Limbaugh, Mark R. Levin, Michael Savage, and Glenn Beck, to shape the public sphere's understanding of issues, Sanchez says they are "worryingly untethered from reality as the impetus to satisfy the demand for red meat overtakes any motivation to report accurately."[4]

One result of this saturated hostile takeover of the American mediated mind is the denigration of serious—and entirely reasonable—mainstream conservative thought. I am a liberal, but that hasn't prevented me from admiring, but disagreeing with, Richard Weaver's 1948 classic *Ideas Have Consequences,*[5] wherein the fall of Western civilization began with a turn away from "one truth" and can be regained only by recognizing that democracy is a matter of existential choice predicated on the maintenance of hierarchies and discrimination. Or from reading, but disagreeing with, William Buckley's *Man and God at Yale*; yes, campuses are full of liberal, "godless" academics, but our job is not to indoctrinate youth but to open their minds to ways of thinking that are, indeed, out of the mainstream. More recently, I am largely in agreement with the reading of conservative intellectual history offered by George H. Nash's "Reappraising the Right,"[6] but believe the three principles he offers—freedom, virtue, and safety—are better attained from a liberal rather than libertarian perspective. So, no, I do not hold to the wrongheaded notion that there are not conservative intellectuals nor that their ideas shouldn't be taken seriously. But, as Stephen F. Hayward, senior fellow at the American Enterprise Institute, put it in an interview with Patricia Cohen: "Conservative intellectuals are in eclipse at the moment."[7]

And why is that? Is it mere coincidence that the national rhetoric has been so divisive, that the Tea Party movement blossomed,

and that a host of other fringe-inspired hot-button issues—
from the Birthers to social justice to immigration to health care
reform—has added narrative fuel to the flames of conservative
fires during the one hundred-plus months of the consecutive reign
of Fox Entertainment News as the top-rated cable news station in
America?[8] As a student of political rhetoric and history it's no surprise to me that far-right propaganda works as an agent of change.
As an interested observer of how the media—on the left and on
the right—has been instrumental in generating interest in topics
and swaying public opinion, I am not surprised by what I have seen
emerge since the election of Barack Obama. What I am surprised
by is the "perfect narrative storm" made by political rhetoric and
right-wing media when in confluence with each other in a time of
economic crisis. What that storm threatens to produce is worth
talking about.

Second, a lot of what we see happening in America now has happened before. There has been a predictable right wing backlash
after the election of every Democratic president during my lifetime, and certainly before that. The difference this time around
has everything to do with that "perfect narrative storm" and our
economy. What the right sells is fear; what Obama preaches is
hope. Fear is the rhetorical tool best suited to the conservative
vision because it posits a world of chaos and disorder enabled by
liberals who have turned away from God and whose decadent ways
threaten to ruin our country, pervert our values, take our guns, rob
us of individual choice and freedom, and disestablish our way of life.
Hope, by contrast, will have none of that. Hope is about an absence
of fear. It is about tolerating diverse opinions and ways of life but
coming together as a people to attain the progress that has defined
America as a world leader in civil rights, economic development,
and global security.

As I say, this isn't new. The far right has threatened the narrative stability, equality, and real security of this country off and on

for a long time. I am old enough to recall the open hate preached by the John Birch Society in its heyday, and my mother and father suffered the cold war threats and innuendo of McCarthyism of the 1950s. Before that my grandmother, a garment union organizer in West Virginia, fought back against politicians and mill owners who used the same strategies of fear and intimidation to prop up their conservative politics and candidates.

Furthermore, what is happening in this "perfect narrative storm," this ideological "war of ideas," is also not restricted to America. The rabble-rousing of far-right extremists in the United States in many ways mirrors similar disturbing political movements alive and well in the United Kingdom, Switzerland, Austria, Russia, Hungry, and Israel just to mention a few. So ours is not a unique political situation; it is merely *our* political situation. But the good news is that what we may learn from our political situation—and from the recovery of our core narrative and the success of a counter-narrative campaign—will likely be useful to liberal allies elsewhere.

Finally, I am a communication scholar. My interest in narratives, the language and rhetoric of them, the distribution of them via media and the Internet, predisposes me to see our world as constructed out of words and actions that I read as forms of communication. I don't consider myself a political scientist, or a historian of politics. I write as a communication scholar with a particular interest in narrative. For this reason, you will not find much polling data or a historiography of politics in these chapters. What you will find is a communication scholar's perspective on a core political narrative that confronts us on a daily basis. And out of that "stuff," that booming, buzzing, bombast of Americana, I will show how and why we should be deeply troubled by this narrative. So much so, that it is now our task to reclaim the American narrative from the radical extremist right.

One of my colleagues asked me why I didn't include more examples of far-left extremism in this book. The simple answer is

that the far-left in America is not armed or particularly dangerous. They pose no direct threat to the United States. In part this
is because they have marginalized themselves with extreme claims
that are easily interpreted as scorn for, if not hatred of, our country.
No one I know outside of the academy takes them very seriously.
In many ways this is an unfortunate truth because some leading
far-left thinkers and spokespersons are intelligent and articulate,
their causes are just, and because some of what they say has merit
regardless of your politics. While I may use far-left examples when
I teach, they are largely absent from this volume because my purpose in writing it is to awaken academics of all persuasions, and the
general reading public, to the clear and present danger posed by
far-right extremists. They *are* armed and as serious in their extremist intentions as any leader of the Taliban.

My sincere hope is that you will join me in this rhetorical
fight against them, this battle of narratives to counter what is fast
becoming, from their point of view and in their own words, an
American jihad.

There are other books, good books and bad books, with similar political goals. What makes this one different is the primary audience I
intend this book to reach. Left Coast Press is an academic publishing
house and its readers, fans, and customers are primarily students and
professors. I am addressing *us*, first and foremost, because I think the
communication and organizing strategies I offer are best deployed
initially on college campuses, places where public debates are encouraged and classes are held on vital issues of the day.

I fully embrace the idea that change begins with the young. I
accept that the motivation for them to lead the charge for change
requires us "village elders" to offer them a better core narrative
with which to organize their own lives as well as the lives and
political activities of others in their communities. It is our job to
provide them with what Kenneth Burke calls "equipment for living," and that includes theories and methods capable of helping

them make sense of everyday life in our hypermediated and highly contested world.

In this way, I am one of those "liberal college professors" that the right rails against. I'm proud of it. And yet, despite fitting the description, I doubt that many students would read me that way (see chapter 5). In my classes I strive to always teach my subject matter in a fair and balanced way. I emphasize scholarship, not politics. And despite the fears of the right about "indoctrinating the youth" with poisonous liberal ideas, I prefer to educate the youth about how ideas are organized, how they are argued, how they are made into stories, and what the better choices are for countering extremism and propaganda.

Probably that is what the right *should* fear.

So let's get started ...

Acknowledgements

This book was written out of conversations I've enjoyed with many people over a number of years. To thank all of them would tax both my memory and the page length of this manuscript. Suffice it to say that all of my interlocutors on the left and on the right—past and present—are alive in my heart, and no doubt their views, their questions, their concerns are everywhere in this volume. To them I say a humble "thank you."

For this specific project there are a few folks I want to single out. From the time I announced this project on my website (www. hlgoodall.com) and on Facebook I have had enthusiastic support and critical commentary from a wide variety of friends, colleagues, and family. Clarence Bray, Jin Brown, Pamela McWherter, Mitch Allen, Norm Denzin, Tori Bray, Harvey Wiener, Stew Auyash, Sarah Tracy, and Richard "Bennett" Furlow all read the first draft either in part or in whole, and offered sage advice, editing suggestions, and encouragement. Thanks to Melanie Mills for a suggested reading that led to the title. To Hugh Downs, for his encouragement. And to Connie Kaplan for advice about the need to cleanse ourselves of narrative toxins found at the end of the first chapter.

My colleagues in the Consortium for Strategic Communication (CSC), in particular Angela Trethewey, Steve Corman, and Jeff Halverson, all worried me with their shared concern that this book would be seen as just another liberal professor's diatribe, and/ or that my use of theoretical materials from our Office of Naval Research (ONR) study of Islamist extremist narratives would be seen by our sponsor as "too political" for our own good. I assured them, as I assure you, that while I am open to both charges being at least somewhat true, I hope I have produced something more thoughtful than a diatribe and that my off-the-ONR-clock application of what I learned from our study is usefully applied to right wing American extremist narratives. I believe that the safety and security of our country benefit from such an analysis. And, of course, I take full responsibility for my views, which do not, in fact, reflect the considered opinion of either my colleagues in the CSC or the United States Navy's Office of Naval Research.

Once again I am thankful for the sponsorship of my editor, Mitch Allen, and the good folks at Left Coast Press, for not only agreeing to publish this contentious volume, but also for making it a better book. I am grateful to Michael and Hannah Jennings for carefully proofreading, copyediting, laying out the pages, and making helpful suggestions for improvement along the way. I am also grateful for Karen Stewart's eye-catching cover, which she completed while prepping for her successful doctoral dissertation defense.

I especially want to thank my wife, Sandra, who will no doubt tell you that she gave me many of the good ideas that made it into this book and argued me out of some bad ones that didn't. She's right about all of that. As an American historian she reminded me of precedents and pointed me in the specific direction of several key sources that helped me advance my case. For twenty years she has been my constant political commentator, lover, wife, editor, and best friend. This book is dedicated to her because it couldn't have been written without her.

And neither would it have been done without Nic, our son, whose very life and hope for his future inspire me every day to want this country, this beautiful idea called America, to be his nation of opportunity, equality, peace, poetry, and justice.

Thanks to all of you ...

Before We Begin ...

In 2004 George Lakoff published a little book called *Don't Think of an Elephant: Know Your Values and Frame the Debate*. The basic premise of it was that Republicans frame important issues as would a Strict Father while Democrats frame their sense of those same issues as Family Members, a notion that echoes what conservative columnist David Brooks observed: that the Republicans are Daddies and the Democrats are Mommies.

Lakoff uses this binary opposition rooted in the family (Father/ Mother) to encourage us to rethink and reframe our fundamental understanding of how progressives should debate conservatives. He produces a summary chart that highlights the basic differences between us:[1]

Progressives	Conservatives
Stronger America	Strong Defense
Broad Prosperity	Free Markets
Better Future	Lower Taxes
Effective Government	Smaller Government
Mutual Responsibility	Family Values

His hope was to deeply influence the Democratic Party leadership. He was successful. Howard Dean, then the chairman of the Democratic Party, summed up the book this way: "If only the Democrats had read George Lakoff a few years ago, we might not be in the position we find ourselves today: out of power in the White House, out of power in Congress, and out of power in the Courts."[2]

Well, here we are in 2010. We are in power in the White House, in control of Congress, and getting closer to even in the Courts. Lakoff's arguments and his attempts to train Democrats to understand that *language* is important in politics certainly paid off. Lakoff himself points out what works within Obama's use of language is what he calls "The Obama Code," which is a moral vision that remains both powerful and ambiguous but that listeners "get."[3] It is fashioned from the following themes:

1. Values Over Programs

2. Progressive Values are American Values

3. Biconceptualism and the New Bipartisanship

4. Protection and Empowerment

5. Morality and Economics Fit Together

6. Systemic Causation and Systemic Risk

7. Contested Concepts and Patriotic Language

8. It's Us, Not Just Him

In other words, it's not just about finding the right metaphors. The Obama Code is about two things: (1) turning progressive ideas and values into actions, and (2) motivating audiences to understand the above collective themes by referencing individual *stories*.

How does he do that? What is his narrative? How does it define a progressive view of America?

Obama assumes, as progressives do, that all of us want a better quality of life. In fact, some of us already have it, and all of us know it. That better quality of life includes a higher standard of living, better health care, greater educational and economic opportunity, a sustainable environment, safe neighborhoods and secure communities. So, for example, when candidate Obama campaigned for the presidency and talked about health care reform, he repeatedly advocated the idea that all Americans deserve to have the same quality of care that is enjoyed by members of the Congress of the United States. It was—and is—a simple idea to grasp: we want, or should want, what they have. But this message was not about adding additional benefits to a much-feared Democratic welfare state. Instead, he argued, if we have the same plan as Congress, our government will save money. Furthermore, Obama did not promise a "give away" of free health care; instead, he combined the idea of health care equity for all people with the economic obligation to ask each and every one of us to pay for it.

These are lofty progressive ideas. They were and are attacked as representing the leftist/socialist/Canadian/French/fascist model. The people doing the attacking, of course, were and are those who already have health care plans, but those of us who study communication have known for a long time that the "rhetoric of confrontation" is always created by a radical division of the "haves" and the "have-nots."[4] Obama's genius is to not only recognize that necessity but to use his repertoire of rhetorical skills to add a powerful second step: motivating audiences by referencing individual stories.

Barack Obama tells us stories we may not want to hear, born as they are in conflict (the have-nots' unfair, often unrecognized sorrow), but what makes them work is that Obama's ultimately work out well for the characters—the average everyday people, the heroes—in them. These are good stories, stories that we want to believe in, and stories that are firmly rooted in progressive ideas and values. This is not a new device. Political stories often feature individuals and their struggles, their hopes, their lives, and their dreams, but Obama offers a new twist by highlighting the ways the government can help people who are struggling to achieve their goals. They are powerful personal narratives, such as this one about the need for health care reform, told on February 4, 2009:

> When Gregory Secrest, from Martinsville, Virginia, lost his job back in August, his kids lost their health care. When he broke the news to his family, his nine-year-old son handed over his piggy bank with $4 in it, and told him, "Daddy, if you need it, you take it."
>
> This is not who we are. We are not a nation that leaves struggling families to fend for themselves. No child in America should

be receiving her primary care in the emergency room in the middle of the night. No child should be falling behind at school because he can't hear the teacher or see the blackboard. I refuse to accept that millions of our kids fail to reach their full potential because we fail to meet their basic needs. In a decent society, there are certain obligations that are not subject to tradeoffs or negotiation—health care for our children is one of those obligations.[5]

We want to believe that we are "a decent society." We want to provide for our children and families. Obama's narrative balances between those values and the way he wants us, as progressives, to think about using government to do that work. Collectively, these stories add up to a new *muscular* liberal narrative. Nothing is free. We all contribute. For all of us to benefit, all of us must pay.

Progressives inherently believe that people should care about each other, and that we are all part of the same human community. That we are a government "for the people." Historically, we have used the power of the federal government to be the force of change that freed the slaves, championed the vote and promoted civil rights, protected children, defended our country in times of war, and that today believes in social justice, and supports—without a single Republican vote in the Senate—the health care reform bill.

We are the people who also believe that our freedom, our liberty, our democracy, and our place in the world are best guaranteed by reason and the rule of law. Ours is an ideology forged in the Enlightenment, hardened by experience, and deepened every time we see those values abused. We hold fast to the idea that our character as a nation is shaped by the values and by the activities of all its people. That our strength in the world is tied to the quality of life we provide to our citizens, the quality of education we offer our children, and our clear and unequivocal support for innovation, whether that innovation is expressed through free enterprise, the sciences, or the arts.

We believe that attaining the American ideal of community for all requires sacrifice, hard work, caring for others, and commitment to the improvement of everyone's quality of life. That is the society we want to live in. To accomplish these ends requires intelligence and creativity. It also requires government. It requires a government that fairly taxes individuals and corporations in order to provide more for the collective "we." A government that fuels the engines of the economy and monitors it for any abuse of power, steps in, and stops it. A government that maintains a strong military and diplomatic corps. In its totality, realizing our American Dream requires nothing more or less than a government that functions to organize economic and social programs that "provide for the common defense and promote the general welfare." It is this government, one enabled and empowered by a great American story that works for all of us, that underscores the progressive version of The American Dream.

At the heart of this progressive narrative of America is a *muscular liberalism* that President Obama excites and that we have not seen so fully embodied since John F. Kennedy. It's a muscular liberalism about *reclaiming the narrative* about our country from those who have, since 1980, appropriated and distorted it. And who tell—and who *believe*—a very different story.

Ronald Reagan famously articulated this alternative version of the story in 1980. It is a story that has deep roots in our culture and has a bloodline running straight through the political DNA of conservatives back to the Revolutionary War: "The fear of centralized power and the belief that free states are fragile and degenerate easily into tyrannies unless diligently protected by a free, knowledgeable, and uncorrupted electorate working through institutions that balance and distribute rather than concentrate power."[6]

Here is The American Dream that is one part "shining city on a hill" and two parts "rags to riches." It combines a fundamentalist moral surety with a rugged individualism, and spins a story of "who we are" around those five conservative themes that Lakoff identified: small government, lower taxes, strong defense, free markets, and family values. The "hero" of this version of the American story is (most recently) "Joe the Plumber," an average God-fearing working guy who is not terribly bright but means well, and who can be relied on to speak truth to power. He owns his own small business, takes care of himself and his family, does pretty well, but could do a whole lot better if the government would get off his back, stop regulating his industry and lower his taxes. Joe's wife, let's call her Mary, is largely silent and absent from this narrative. Probably she is home tending 2.5 kids and making a low-fat dinner. In the evenings she does the books for Joe's business and helps the kids with their homework. That is the dream version.

But Joe and Mary aren't entirely pleased with the way things are. In fact, they are both pretty angry. Why? Because America is changing and they don't like what they see. The reality rather than dream is what they are living. They have watched as their standard of living eroded and rather than second guess their own choices or the leaders they helped to elect, they look outwardly for someone to blame. For Joe and Mary and a legion of loyal Republicans, it was not the failed economic policies of the Reagan, Bush, and Bush II administrations, but *Liberals* who are responsible. Liberals want to socialize our country. They want to raise taxes to support "those less fortunate," which is really just a Commie-code for those too lazy to work, or illegal immigrants who are taking our jobs, or the homeless who don't really deserve to live. Look what liberals did for the Blacks. And now one of them is president. Plus, most liberals don't believe in God. Neither did Stalin. Liberals want to take our guns and provide free abortions. They have no morals. And, as we all know, our kids are exposed to a liberal view of history and culture in public schools that are supported by our taxes! They are taught that Darwin's *theory* of evolution trumps the *Holy Bible*. They are taught that "climate change" is based on real science rather than wild speculation generated to fund liberal causes. They are taught to respect the rights of queers. To let them be open about their perversion in the military, for God's sake. To allow them to marry, which is an affront to what God intended. It was Adam and Eve, not Adam and Steve!

They ask: So what must be done? It's 2010 and the soul of the nation is at stake. We conservatives must unite in our anger and take back the American narrative. We must stand up to, and shout down, the Liberals who are ruining it for us. We are the true Patriots and this is all about protecting our freedoms, our liberty, our mission to let Divine Will Be Done! We *are* the chosen people. We *are* the elect. This is *our* country and we are taking it back!

What we have is two stories, two narrative versions of America. Two visions for the future, not only for our country, but also for our world. With apologies to George Lakoff, it is about far more than just "framing." It is about the stories we want to live in, and *for*. It is a Battle of Narratives in a political war for hearts and minds. What we have are two very different stories of who we are as a people, what the meaning of The American Dream should be, and what an American Dream has to offer and contribute to the world.

I think that the progressive, muscular liberal story is a better one for all of us and especially for our children. And that is what this book is all about.

1. The Battle of Narratives

The history of all hitherto existing society is *not* the history of class struggles, but instead the history of *narrative* struggles. Storytellers, from the creators of hieroglyphics to the inventors of alphabets to the perpetrators of gods and myths, gospels, wars, ideas, science, and *sura*, stood in constant opposition to one another and carried on an uninterrupted, now hidden, now open, battle of narratives, a battle that each time ended either in a revolutionary re-constitution of society at large, or in the common ruin of an old story that once held sway over entire populations and was thought to be true.[1]

For these reasons, we must agree from the outset that this call to narrative engagement, this call to revolution and to the reconstitution of society is dangerous. Why dangerous? Because, in fact and in fiction, there is no more urgent call, no more magical spell, than the spells of well told stories and the irresistible call to identify with powerful core narratives. At the center of this call to reconstitute society through narrative engagement is the dire need for narrative accountability, the right of every free thinking citizen to cry foul when her or his narrative space has been ruptured by bad stories, ideological distortions, misrepresentations and lies, and brazen stupidity passes for reasoned discourse and/or coherent narrative.

What is often lost in these rhetorical flare ups is that the ability to tell a story well does not necessarily mean that the story you hear is *true.* Some of history's monsters were legendary storytellers. Some of today's most egregious violators of our narrative trust are themselves honey-tongued manipulators, talking heads, politicians, and terrorist leaders or spokespersons. And some of these narratives, such as the call to martyrdom used to recruit children to the cause of jihad, strap lethal bombs on themselves in exchange for the promise of seventy-two virgins, and detonate those bombs and their bodies in crowded public spaces because they are told this is what Allah demands, are evidence enough of the enduring lure of powerful narratives and their very real danger.

But those of us who believe in the power of narrative to alter perceptions of reality, to change minds, and to influence choices of action should not be quelled by the fear of the misuses of these powers of persuasion. It is not productive. We understand the problems inherent in any narrative strategy. But that should not stop our advocacy, our campaign for narrative engagement, because there is too much at stake. There, I have posted the requisite ethical and moral caution, you read it, and together we move on.

Consider yourself warned: not only are compelling core narratives dangerous, and narrative engagement with the violent ideological narratives of others dangerous, but also reading this book and acting on its advice is dangerous. It is dangerous because it speaks the truth at a time when the battleground is already prepared, sides have already been chosen, and chaos and disorder are everywhere. The stakes have never been higher nor the fight more worthy. Welcome, brave warrior, to the narrative revolution!

Let us begin this revolution, this reconstitution of society, with a statement of first principles. So first and foremost we are, as Walter Fisher expresses it, *homo narrans*—humans as storytellers.[2] It is our ability to tell stories, and to make lives and cultures out of them, that separates us from all other animals. Mastering this skill, to tell compelling, motivating, and uplifting stories, elevates some gifted storytellers, even those with foreign-sounding names, to the White House, while others, who themselves may also aspire to high office or higher status or perhaps just a tenured professorship somewhere preferably not in the Midwest, don't realize their dreams.

This is because those less narratively equipped among us, although they may be just as good-looking, but who are less able to invent rhetorical visions capable of inspiring listeners, less able to poetically organize and authentically deliver them—people who, for example, jot down talking points with felt markers on their palm—are those persons who are often and—let us not mince words here—unkindly considered to be dumb-asses,[3] by comparison.

Those who rise to the challenges of reclaiming the narrative do not suffer dumb-asses gladly. We define as a common enemy the 29 percent of Americans who believe that a "hillbilly palmpilot"[4] deserves a crack at the White House. Those 29 percent are no doubt dumb-asses, too. Or, in a poll released the day after the first House passage of the health care reform bill, of the overheated denizens of this right-wing ideological swamp:

- 67 percent of Republicans (and 40 percent of Americans overall) believe that Obama is a socialist.

- 57 percent of Republicans (32 percent overall) believe that Obama is a Muslim.

- 45 percent of Republicans (25 percent overall) agree with the Birthers in their belief that Obama was "not born in the United States and so is not eligible to be president."

- 38 percent of Republicans (20 percent overall) say that Obama is "doing many of the things that Hitler did."

- Scariest of all, 24 percent of Republicans (14 percent overall) say that Obama "may be the Antichrist."[5]

But the dumb-asses are right about one thing: we are living right now at the crossroads of a righteous narrative struggle for the very soul of America. It is being waged daily between those of us who believe that intelligent leadership enhanced by a credible and poetic narrative is preferable to leadership by inarticulate dumb-asses. It is being waged daily by educators who believe that the future of the world depends on the stories we tell about what truly matters in life, about peace, about social justice, about the eradication of poverty, disease, and ignorance, instead of the corrupt ideology of business schools and conservative Republicans that teaches its students to value only greed, the accumulation of personal wealth, and the ruthless spirit of advanced absentee-owner capitalism that is spread through their books and given public voice on Fox News and the *Wall Street Journal*.

This is the enemy who is near. This is the enemy who is also well financed. This is the enemy who is selling an old story that divides the world into those who believe in a literal interpretation of the Constitution and the Holy Bible, and those who maintain that these narratives must be understood within their historical contexts and with a clear view of the consequences that are entailed by a literal reading. They want to take our country back to the polite white values and lifestyle of the mid-eighteenth century and, if possible, refight the Civil War. States rights, not federal rights. No taxes on profits. No health care reform. No equality for women. No minimum wage, which is, of course, only another way of saying "wage slavery." And so forth.

The enemy wants to restore the Reagan Caliphate. They want to abolish support for public education by lowering taxes as well as lessening teachers' salaries. Why? Because an educated public is likely to become a critical public. A critical public will be attuned to the lack of sound reasoning. A critical public will not respond favorably to a lack of respect for scientific knowledge. Or history. And so it is that conservatives have declared war on education. You know why. Because a critical public capable of easily recognizing "plainfolks propaganda" passing for truth is the last thing the enemy needs or wants.

The enemy is a clear and present danger to our preferred American way of life. And this enemy has a loud voice and controls big corporations, most of the votes in both political parties, and all the conservative media. But make no mistake. The near enemy is, collectively, nothing less than a radical extremist narrative and as we saw with the Oklahoma City bombing no less an imminent threat than our enemies living an ocean or more away.

Narratives endorsing violent extremism are spreading. It's not just the dumb-asses in the 29 percent that we need to counter. It is their influence over the young, the future generations. For this battle of narratives is destined to be an enduring war, and if you agree to be part of our revolution, understand that you are volunteering for the long haul.

Narratives, Fisher teaches us, must do two things well: they must "hang together" as narratives and they must "ring true" for audiences. Narrative probability and narrative fidelity are the cornerstones of narrative power. For too long the old left—our academic and professional left, the brothers and sisters of this revolution—failed both tests of narrative power. For too long, those of us who see the world differently than our enemies do have been divided among ourselves by allegiance to a diverse array of smaller stories and as a result have lost our way back to a common storyline.

Instead, ours has been a meandering multivocal political folktale teetering on the brink of narrative incoherence. It's like an overreaching ambitious novel of American life that tries to be about everything and as a result becomes confusing and contentious and loses the interest of readers and listeners, which is what has happened to the far left.

We have also burdened our story with the theme of pride in our moral superiority. No one likes *hubris*. And—this is key—we have written our narrative of America—the land of hope and opportunity, of freedom and dreams—with an infinite sadness punctuated with dysfunctional Congressional fecklessness and inefficiency and our resulting public despair.

Tell me honestly, how is this version of our nation, much less our revolutionary mission, at all narratively satisfying? It is *not* satisfying. It is boring. It is weak. It is a tale of woe. Of powerlessness. Of futility. We have become like the old drunk at the corner bar quoting John F. Kennedy and Martin Luther King, Jr.; some people feel sorry for him but no one is really listening to him. Not anymore.

That left—the old guard left—had its narrative chance and blew it. It gave up on a great storyline in exchange for special interest politics and political correctness, neither of which made most Americans identify with the narrators or want to know what happens next. But it did make a lot of them turn the page. And open another book. The

Book of Reagan, illustrated by George Herbert Walker Bush and narrated by George W. Bush.

The lesson about narrative that those of us on the left must learn begins with a question: does our current tale of woe *hang together*? The answer is: no. There are too many small stories crowding out the larger narrative. The antidote is President Obama's commitment to progressive ideas and values that allow for diverse local interpretations of meaning, thereby empowering all of our special interest camps to identify with it without explicitly saying so.

The second lesson also begins with a question: does our tale of woe *ring true*? To answer that question I have to ask another, analogous one: *how many academics does it take to screw in a light bulb?* This very question was recently posted to a department email listserv by Dan Canary, a colleague of mine, and I reprint below the responses he gave:

> *Answer:* Well, that answer depends on one's theoretic perspective!
>
> For example:
>
> *For an empiricist:* At least three—one to screw it in and two others to assess intercoder reliability;
>
> *For an interpretivist:* One would first need to know the social construction of what it means to screw in a lightbulb;
>
> *For an ethnographer:* S/he would sit in the dark to understand the culture of the room;
>
> *For an autoethnographer:* S/he would sit in the dark, then write about her/his experience;
>
> *For a critical cultural person:* Damn the hegemonic lightbulb company that has power over the means to see!

I had to add to it. So I wrote back a couple of small corrections to two of the entries:

> *For the ethnographer:* S/he would sit in the dark waiting for an opportunity to interview the empiricist, the interpretivist, the autoethnographer, and the critical cultural person, meanwhile collecting notes about the culture of

the dark room and wondering why some people insist on light, anyway.

For the autoethnographer: S/he would sit in the dark, then write about the experience, discovering along the way that s/he was the light bulb.

See the analogy? Of course you do. Our love of diverse theoretical orientations and methods has damned us academics to an empty pluralism. Just as its love of diverse causes damned the left to behave much as warring tribes behave in a civil war. We have been committed to our own individual and separate causes so long that we believe we are the light bulb instead of remembering that it was—and is—our job to screw in the light bulb so that we bring light to everyone in the room. We have given up our core narrative (see chapter 5) in favor of celebrating a collectivity of worthy causes that makes the core of what we stand for seem virtually incoherent. Making the disjointed weak narrative of the left oh so easy to attack from the right.

Enter Obama's second rhetorical principle, which happens to be a lesson I teach students about good writing: *stories drive the information.*[6] Not the other way around. Stories, such as the one I used earlier from Obama about the boy offering his uninsured father his money, open up listeners and readers to the harder content, to statistics, and to policies. *Stories drive the information.* Not the other way around. In our quest for a better liberal narrative, a muscular liberal core narrative, we must remember that.

For those who accept the challenge of this book, it falls to us to collectively amass our diverse resources and locate a narrative capable of leading us, and the world, out of the dark room made darker every day by the enemies' creeping ignorance and greed that have brought on our economic, social, and institutional decay. We must find a common narrative that both hangs together and rings true, without requiring extended, competitive, conflicted, and hand-wringing debates over how we screw in a light bulb.

We have the power of an alternative narrative on our side. President Obama proved that with his election and again with successful health care reform. Against all odds he proved that the power of a narrative of hope and change based on a compelling story and good reasons can and does trump the politics of fear, as well as change history. But he cannot do it alone. His *narrative* cannot do it alone. We must help him overcome the paralyzing fear and anxiety that far right Republicans and Teabaggers promote. We must collectively help America overcome the fear and war rhetoric the previous administration manipulated to maintain their power and promote a binary vision of the world. That narrative defined America and the West as the cowboy Crusaders bent on once again conquering the world.

That right wing narrative fueled racial and religious differences at home and abroad.

That narrative contributed nothing to the Gross National Product but increased by tenfold our debt, and our children's debt.

That narrative failed to keep us safe or secure, for although the Bush minions like to gloss over it, 9/11 did occur on their watch.

That narrative brought our economy, indeed the world's economy, to its knees while protecting the million dollar bonuses of criminal billionaires and their Harvard Business School lackeys.

And then, Ta Da!, the gang that scared us into two wars and near economic collapse became the party that gave us Sarah Palin, the cheerleader of the dumb, as a serious candidate for the vice presidency of the United States? That endorses the extremist views of the Teabaggers? No! My sentiments echo those of fellow progressive, Michael Seitzman:

> Bipartisanship can kiss my ass. Seducing, pleasing and appeasing the current Republican Party is as interesting to me as lopping off an arm. These people have allowed themselves to be taken over by extremists, imbeciles, racists, fear-mongers and ignorant thugs. They choose circus politics over good policy, the popularity of the mediocre and incompetent over responsibility, intelligence and common sense. The Republican political bible begins with the god Karl Rove, exalts cartoon prophets like George W. Bush, Michele Bachmann and Sarah Palin, and demands its disciples receive

communion from lunatic priests Rush Limbaugh and Glenn Beck. The Right laughably and transparently throws around euphemistic bumper-sticker words like "small government" and "socialism" to thinly disguise their real agenda to relieve your conscience of any inconvenient feelings of responsibility toward your fellow humans.[7]

If you are not yet angry, you are not a true brother or sister of our cause. This is not a battle for passive aggressive liberals who hedge their bets, mute their anger, or fail to step up to the narrative battle-field. That sort of liberal is no longer credible, no longer worthy of the narrative paradigm.

Yet our anger is not enough, nor is it often directed against our true enemy: the far right. Instead, as has been our habit for decades, the left tends to direct its anger not at our true enemies, but instead at our own leaders. We want them to be perfect liberals in an imperfect political world. We want them to instantly address our particular grievances, make policies to justify our causes, and otherwise use the power of the presidency as an axe rather than a scalpel. This is unrealistic and, frankly, boneheaded. It is the cry for vengeance from the child on the playground who has been bullied, but it is not a reasoned response nor is it likely to achieve the desired policy ends. Yes, we must stand up to playground bullies. Yes, we must hold them accountable for their actions. And yes, we need policies to prevent others from behaving that way and getting away with it. But as long as we focus on bullies and cry for their blood, we fail to look at the bigger picture. We fail to see that bullies are not born, but made, enabled by cultural and social circumstances, by poverty, neglect and abuse. By cuts in funding to schools that prevent hiring trained professionals to deal with behavioral and psychological problems. By cuts in funding to schools that increase class sizes and by cuts in funding by states to social services that include police and social workers. Or by unemployment that tears at the fabric of affected families. Or by a number of other challenges to a just, democratic society that are part and parcel of the problem to be solved. In other words, while we are angry at the bully, we must remain focused on the future we want to live in, that larger, better world we, as united progressives, can bring about.

In this regard, is it any wonder that White House Press Secretary, Robert Gibbs, on August 10, 2010, unleashed criticism at what he calls "the professional left"? This is a presidency that has passed more new legislation than any other since FDR. As Larry Berman, professor of political science and expert on the presidency at the University of California-Davis, observes:

> The irony, of course, is that Gibbs's frustration reflects the fact that the conservative opposition has been so effective at undermining the president's popular approval.... And from Gibbs's perspective, and the White House perspective, they ought to be able to catch a break from people who, in their view, should be grateful and appreciative.[8]

While that last sentiment is certainly true, it misses a critical point. In fact, one major reason why the left has been so motivated to criticism, and also why many progressives have found fault with Obama's leadership, is due not so much to a failure to address critical policy issues. It is a *failure to articulate and disseminate an overarching narrative* capable of countering thirty years of brainwashing and propaganda from the right on the singular issue of the need for good government. Until that narrative washes clean the rhetorical debris that empowers the far right and infects even moderate Republicans and centrists from both parties, the criticism will continue and this presidency will be in jeopardy.

As I say, the stakes in this Battle of Narratives are high.

Narratives about revolutions, about the reconstitution of society, are dangerous, politically dangerous, and because they are dangerous they require writers and speakers, as well as those who would oppose them, to take risks.[9] There are many ways to take risks with narratives, and not all of those risks, nor even necessarily the best ones, involve putting yourself, or others, in harm's way. But some risks do. And that is the price of having let things go on badly for so long.

I say this because during the recent health care reform debates the behavior of leaders of the minority party attained a level of righteous wrongness that could only happen because we let them get away with defining their values as the true American values for so long. Unchallenged by a credible alternative narrative until President Obama came along, Republican leaders and far right wing nutjob followers simply did not accept the outcome of the 2008 presidential election. Their leaders, with a wink and nod, implied that they might not control the White House (only a temporary condition, they assured followers), but they would control Congress by blocking any attempt the Democrats made to enact the changes that Obama was elected to implement. As James Zogby put it:

> The idea that the minority party represents the "will of the people" (not some of the people, but "the people") is the seedling of a totalitarian mindset. In this mindset—democracy doesn't matter, ideas are not to be discussed, and opposing views are not to be respected. What matters is that they alone have truth, they alone are metaphysically connected to the "mind of the people" and can interpret their will, and because they have truth and speak for the people, others represent a threat and must be silenced and stopped.[10]

As the debate drew to an end, these "Hatriots" and their followers spewed vindictive, threatened the lives of those who disagreed with them, threatened to assassinate the president, and began hurling bricks through windows at Democratic Party offices across the country. To wit:

> First there are the insensate attacks on those who dare to disagree with the party's views led by the Republican minority leader John Boehner in his final remarks last night assailing the health reform legislation. Then there are the Republicans who cheered on the hatred and ire of the Teabagger protesters encircling the capital from the balcony of the House of Representatives over the weekend. Then there are the Teabaggers themselves who hurled racial and homophobic slurs at various Democratic Party legislators.
>
> And what about the vitriol mouthed through the months without any Republican regrets by the right-wing radio hosts like Glenn Beck, Bill O'Reilly, Sean Hannity and their cadres. All of this—hatred, churlishness, pique, resentment, snarling,

incivility—has become the face of a political party which once reflected the sunny optimism of Ronald Reagan.[11]

Make no mistake: the far right politics currently embraced wholeheartedly by sitting Republicans and supported by commentators and talk show hosts is not going to shut up. Nor are they going to give up. They think they are right. *Extremely* right.

I think they are dangerous extremists. I call them "the near enemy."

The enemy we know is the near enemy. This the narrative wolf howling at the front door. This the narrative wolf characterized by Timothy Egan as "those rage-filled partisans with spittle on their lips."[12] This wolf is howling for the return of the Reagan Caliphate. The true believer bloodline that runs from their prophet through two burning Bushes and right into the cold "Mamma Grizzly" heart of Sarah Palin. Or Scott Brown. Or Michele Bachmann. Or Someone Else, yet to emerge.

But there is also a far enemy that threatens our way of life. That threatens the whole of our country. That is the narrative constructed by violent extremists abroad. That is the narrative that most people on the left have conveniently ignored, or at least have allowed the far right to own. And own *badly*. It is the narrative wolf howling at our back door. And I am here to tell you that it is a powerful narrative that we on the left can no longer afford to ignore.

The far enemy's narrative goes something like this:[13] the world is corrupt and in chaos, and the nations of the Arab and Muslim world have fallen from the path of True Islam. These Arab and Muslim states exist in a state of pagan heresy or ignorance similar to what existed on the Arabian Peninsula at the time of Islam's birth, a state of *jahaliyya*. What is needed is a return to True Islam, a restoration of the Caliphate, and the imposition of rule by Sharia law. To do that, those who engage in holy jihad must first end the evil influences of the West and rid the land of the foreign occupiers—the American crusaders and their allies. To do that may require martyrdom.

Here are some questions everyone needs to ask about the far enemy's narrative: Why is it that the appeal of the Salafi and Wahhabi schools of thought, each preaching a return to the values and lifestyle of seventh century Islam, has grown enormously in popularity? How is it that otherwise ordinary law abiding Muslims identify with a social movement that defines as enemies of God not only all apostate leaders of Arab and Muslim nations, but also Christians and Jews as well as those who call themselves Muslims but who do not follow in the fundamentalist ways of the Salafi and Wahhabi creed? Or who learn to define their lives as meaningful only within a web of a significance tied to a return to the ummah and to a reinstatement of the Caliphate dissolved by Kemmal Ataturk in 1924?

Or, finally, what is it about their narrative, a global social narrative that defines the West, and particularly America, as the enemy, as the Crusader, as the evil that can only be eradicated by a holy jihad, so much so that the goal of this system of stories has been their recruitment into an ideological alliance with a cause that preaches the love of death and the inevitability of victory?

It is worth noting that one root cause of both extremist narratives is a narrow view of the relationship of politics to religion and its reliance on a literal interpretation of a particular sacred text. In both cases, these extremist narratives want to return to a distant past, not move forward into the future. And in both cases, the call to action involves extreme, violent actions against anyone who would challenge them on religious grounds or stand in their political way.

The reason the far enemy's narrative has potency is clear. It is because as a narrative it is coherent to those who hear it, it connects to a view of history they know and do not question, it offers them meaningful work—the work of Allah—and it contains a powerful message that not only rings true, but that also compels ideological identification, personal sacrifice, and extreme actions.[14] Sound familiar?

Ye who have lost all hope, enter here.

Ye who have a life, an education, a spouse, children, you, too, enter here.

This fidelity to a great cause, a righteous cause, is the basic appeal of the far enemy's narrative. It offers close personal identification for listeners and readers, and it asks what you will do, what you will personally contribute, to want to find out what happens next.

It is, so far at least, better than our American narrative because our American narrative keeps changing. Is this a war fought for revenge against al-Qaeda for 9/11? Or is it about oil? Did we invade Iraq because there were weapons of mass destruction or because we thought Saddam Hussein was an evil dictator who threatened stability in the region? Has our presence there made the region more stable or has it been a destabilizing influence? And why are we now leaving Iraq to once again enter Afghanistan? Is it to finally get bin Laden or is it to end the rule of the Taliban? Is propping up a corrupt regime there that will likely fall as soon as we leave worth the investment of American lives and a billion or so dollars every day?

Why were we in Vietnam?

What are we doing in Afghanistan today?

We've lost the narrative thread. But at least Chairman of the Joint Chiefs Admiral Mike Mullen and Secretary of Defense Robert Gates figured out the fundamental problem. They say this: *Since we cannot kill our way to victory, we must win the battle of narratives.*

This most recent "overseas contingency operation" is not just another campaign to win hearts and minds, which is what we need to wage here at home against the narrative wolf at the front door. But for the far enemy, the wolf howling at our back door and all whom they would influence with their storyline worldwide, ours must be a campaign to win hearts and *souls.*

One more observation. These two narrative wolves are related. It's not America—the beautiful idea of it—that the jihadists hate. It is, from their point of view, the hypocrisy and corruption and chaos of our policies. It is, from their point of view, our inability or unwillingness to live up to our own ideals and values. It is, for them, our incomprehensible separation of Church and State. And this message, this storyline, has generated appeal within our homeland. The narrative wolf at the back door has already morphed into the jihadi next door.[15]

This battle of narratives we find ourselves in today, and about which this book is written, is serious business and therefore requires some action. From *you.* This is not some theoretical academic hijinks about which you can sip your latte and just engage intellectually. No. This is the driven stuff of life. This is about power, passion, risk, and cour-age—to speak the narrative truth in story forms, to compel readers and listeners to want to *find out what happens next*. And it is about holding the dumb-asses and the jihadis accountable for their narra-tives, and finding ways to intervene in their terrorist discourse, to dis-rupt it, to prevent it from being used to recruit children and young adults to their idiot ideology.

Nor is this Battle of Narratives a partisan call that excludes those members of the Republican Party or others on the right from joining us. Consider, if you will, well known and highly respected Repubican lawyer Ted Olson's appearance on August 8, 2010, on Fox News defending the defeat of Proposition 8's ban on gay marriage in California. Below is part of that exchange (the link to the video of his appearance may be found in the notes to this chapter):[16]

"Where is the right to same-sex marriage in the Constitution?" asked Wallace.

"Where is the right to interracial marriage in the Constitution, Chris?" replied Olson.

"The Supreme Court has looked at marriage and has said that the right to marry is a fundamental right for all citizens. So you call it interracial marriage and then you could prohibit it, no? The Supreme Court said no. The same thing here," explained Olson.

"The judge after hearing three weeks of testimony and full day of closing arguments and listening to experts from all over the world concluded that the denial of the right to marry to these individuals in California hurt them and did not advance the cause of opposite sex marriage," Olson continued.

"This is what judges are expected to do. It's not judicial activism. It's judicial responsibility in the classic sense."...

"We believe that a conservative value is stable relationships and stable community and loving individuals coming together and forming a basis that is a building block of our society, which includes marriage," said Olson.

Chris Wallace was reduced to silence. Wallace closed the seg-ment by admitting that it was a wonder Ted Olson didn't win all of his

Supreme Court cases. What Olson did was counter the far right narrative on the soundbite "judicial activism" with pure reasoning and a thorough understanding of the Constitution and our history of civil rights in America. He didn't lose his temper. He didn't question the political motives of the Fox News commentator. He stuck to the facts. He argued from knowledge. He supplied a narrative that linked the wisdom of the founding fathers and the history of equal protection under the law to gay marriage.

And that is what more of us, and more Republicans like Olson, need to do.

Are you ready to take some risks with your own narrative? To become dangerous to the demagogues and hate mongerers?

Probably you are wondering what, exactly, I mean by "become dangerous." For too long we citizens and academics have put up with a world of chaos and stupidity created by an addiction to bad stories, political lies, celebrity scandals, reality tv that is anything but real, and a mediated news circus that keeps us fat, ignorant, and thoroughly entertained. Perhaps we thought if we just did our jobs it would all go away. Or if we just raised our kids properly, that was enough. Or that someday, surely, as Bruce Springsteen once put it, a "savior would rise from these streets."

But that hasn't happened. Slowly we became more complicit with the spread of narrative mediocrity, less surprised by scandal and corruption, so much so that we have shown ourselves to be willing to half-way believe just about any nonsense. "These banks are too big to fail," being one example. Or the story told by five members of the Supreme Court when they ruled that opening your wallet and opening your mouth are the same thing. Or that Sarah Palin, candidate for the second highest office in the land and a heartbeat away from the presidency, could see Russia from her house in Alaska.

Are you not sick and tired of this assault on narrative rationality? Are you not ready to join the revolution? Are you not ready to engage the dumb-asses and extremists and turn this battle around?

I propose a nine-point action plan for those who would dare act on their own anger:

1. Purify your own narrative; eliminate the lies you can identify, the selfishness and self-interest that pollute both your soul and the soul of our nation, the corrosive elements in your own speech that work against a civil discourse.

2. Produce and consume only those narratives that matter to the future of the world.

3. Write and read as if your life depends on it.

4. Cultivate knowledge of the near and far enemies, learn their communication strategies and propaganda tactics, and whenever and wherever possible, resist and/or disrupt them.[17]

5. Hold everyone accountable for the stories they tell. Take the time to phone in complaints, contribute to blogs, and write letters to the editor.

6. Talk back to offensive political party organizers and religious zealots who invade your community.

7. Make civic responsibility your job.

8. Join civic responsibility with public scholarship and rethink your research agenda.

9. Cultivate a wider audience for your narratives and allies for your resistance work.

2. Binary Opposites and Narrative IEDs

Our War of Ideas Is a War Fought with Words and Humor

At the very beginning of our quest to reconstitute society through deployment of a progressive narrative, it is imperative to take stock of ourselves, and to understand from our own habits of speech and manner those lies, those sources of selfishness, and those corrosive habits of an uncivil, unproductive discourse that we wish to work against in others. For it is morally impure to engage in The Battle of Narratives, to commit to working to produce a more civil and responsible discourse capable of defeating the near and far enemies of reason, empathy, and the goal of a common goodness, while we ourselves remain tainted.

Some years ago I began this work of self-cleansing when I realized that my own story was composed largely of half-truths, feints of thinking and speaking that left out what I did not want to admit, that I did not dare to know. As a result I was, I realized, internally at war with myself, and these small maneuvers of falsity were designed to repel any attack from the outside that aimed to open me to the truth. I was also untrue to my family. I thought that by closing off those dark scenes from my remembered Cold War childhood and adolescence I could live forever in some abstract better light.

But I was wrong. And indeed, by not fully embracing what philosophers call "the duality of my own spirit," the commingling of good and evil that is in the heart of every one of us, I could never attain that better light. For the light I was seeking needed my comprehension of darkness as much as I needed to learn how to deal with my need for it, and my uses of it.

That journey has been elsewhere recorded, and I'll not recount it here.[1] My purpose in bringing it up is to remind us all that our collective attempt to purify the national narrative begins with an individual commitment to purify our own narrative.

But such work is not always what it appears to be. For as I learned, the act of purification is not about casting off what is hidden or unclean or angry or bitter in memory, but instead the harder work of accepting it, of working with it, of making it part of that greater understanding of the self and our relationship to the Cosmos that we all seek. That acceptance and working with the light and dark sides of the self is what it means to be *authentic*. And only by learning to be authentic can we rise up from a half-lived life of narrative enslavement to narrative freedom. From that vantage, complex and conflicted as it must be, we can then exercise our right of free speech—including our right to be angry in our speech—in a more purposeful manner.

One way to accomplish that end is to recognize that it is the enemies' *in*authenticity that, in part, fuels our collective anger. The leaders of the opposition are hucksters. Frauds. Masters and mistresses of the con. They are in it for the money, for the celebrity, and for the ego. They don't really care about you. Or me. Or our country.

Nica24, on Facebook, passed along this poem that sums up nicely the inauthenticity of even the opposition's anger:

You Didn't Get Mad When

You didn't get mad when the Supreme Court stopped a legal recount and appointed a president.

You didn't get mad when Cheney allowed energy company officials to dictate energy policy.

You didn't get mad when a covert CIA operative got outed.

You didn't get mad when the Patriot Act got passed.

You didn't get mad when we illegally invaded a country that posed no threat to us.

You didn't get mad when we spent over 600 billion (and counting) on said illegal war.

You didn't get mad when over 10 billion dollars just disappeared in Iraq.

You didn't get mad when you found out we were torturing people.

You didn't get mad when the government was illegally wiretapping Americans.

You didn't get mad when we didn't catch Bin Laden.

You didn't get mad when you saw the horrible conditions at Walter Reed.

You didn't get mad when we let a major U.S. city, New Orleans, drown.

You didn't get mad when we gave a 900 billion tax break to the rich.

You didn't get mad when the deficit hit the trillion dollar mark.

You finally got mad when the government decided that people in America deserved the right to see a doctor if they are sick. Yes, illegal wars, lies, corruption, torture, stealing your tax dollars to make the rich richer, are all okay with you, but helping other Americans...oh hell no.[2]

The above lines also reflect a powerful narrative lesson: that the goal of our counter-narrative cannot simply be to "beat the enemy," but to *expose* them. To expose the inauthenticity of their staged performances. To track down their overt lies. To reveal the corruption that runs through their secret or covert lives. To use our freedom of speech and ability to reason to out-argue them, the power of our stories to outclass them, and *our freedom* to network, to pass along, to collectively organize in order to challenge their narrative here, there, and everywhere. To use what Aristotle calls "all the available means of persuasion."

This chapter is dedicated to an investigation of one aspect of that right of free speech and its relationship to anger, that habit of everyday life in the war of ideas at home and abroad that involves what I have learned to call the deployment of binary opposites and "narrative IEDs."[3]

Clancy Sigel, writing in the *Guardian*, wonders where the sane liberal anger has gone? He observes, correctly, that a "sterile politeness" drives everything from the resolution of schoolyard disputes to Obama administration policy debates. He asks: "Where and when did we lefties lose this vital part of our social language?"[4]

We have a narrative challenge to combat these violent extremists among us, but the problem beneath that challenge is largely one of language: how do we give voice to our own anger without succumbing to the same rhetorical style evidenced by the far right? How far do we dare go to counter their craziness without seeming crazy ourselves? And yes, I do mean crazy. Consider this summary statement of the craziness, drawn from a 2010 Frank Rich column in the *New York Times*:

> Such violent imagery and invective, once largely confined to blogs and talk radio, is now spreading among Republicans in public office or aspiring to it. Last year Michele Bachmann, the redoubtable Tea Party hero and Minnesota congresswoman, set the pace by announcing that she wanted "people in Minnesota armed and dangerous" to oppose Obama administration climate change initiatives. In Texas, the Tea Party favorite for governor, Debra Medina, is positioning herself to the right of the incumbent, Rick Perry—no mean feat given that Perry has suggested that Texas could secede from the union. A state sovereignty zealot, Medina reminded those at a rally, that "the tree of freedom is occasionally watered with the blood of tyrants and patriots."[5]

There are many other examples of such violent extremist rhetoric no doubt familiar to you. These explosive uses of language represent what my colleagues Daniel Bernardi and Scott Ruston, studying violent extremist rumors in the Middle East, term "narrative IEDs."[6] Just as in that rugged war-torn landscape "improvised explosive devices" tear apart everything from the local peace to military transport trucks, rumors there are used as weapons of mass persuasion to seed distrust among the population and to cast doubt on the motives of American forces. Because the rumors are generally effective, and because they are difficult if not impossible to counter, they operate as explosive rhetorical devices that disrupt the possibility of meaningful dialogue and mutual trust.

The same could be said of phrases such as those given above. In our rugged political landscape, these narrative IEDs are effective because they combine the mediated political power of the repetitious soundbite with a transparent call to arms that divides citizens from government, the right from the center and certainly from the left, and those who side with their extremist views from anyone else.

Plus, mouthing expressions that sound tough—the tactic of the schoolyard bully—often provides just enough narrative appeal to be confused with actually being tough, which is one way that the weak gain power and influence among those truly vulnerable persons who themselves want desperately to identify with strength. Again, as the spread of an anti-America rumor in Iraq or Afghanistan or Yemen sows seeds of doubt as well as organizes vulnerable local populations against us, so, too, do the narrative IEDs of the violent extremist political right in our country sow seeds of doubt about the integrity of our leadership and at the same time organize populations against it and the rest of us.

For example, in August 2010, right wing media-fueled protests erupted in New York City over the proposed (and approved by the Mayor and by the NYC planning commission) construction of an Islamic Cultural Center near the site of the 9/11 tragedy. The issue was immediately framed as a binary opposition of "us" versus "them" by the right where all too often "us" was defined as "true" Americans, Christians, and patriots who remembered and revered 9/11 and "them" was starkly defined as darker skinned Muslims who had attacked the World Trade Center and, by extension, the whole of Islam in general. Jarret Brachman, director of Cronus Global, a security consulting firm, and author of the book *Global Jihadism*, was quoted in the *Wall Street Journal* as seeing the division in terms of the global war on terror:

> al Qaeda and other groups have long used imagery from the wars in Iraq and Afghanistan to recruit new members. But the U.S. position has been that those wars are not against Islam and that the U.S. has Muslim allies in the fight. Anti-Muslim rhetoric in the U.S is different, since jihadists can use Americans' words to make the case that the U.S. is indeed at war with Islam. The violent postings are not just on al Qaeda-linked websites but on prominent, mainstream Muslim chat forums."[7]

Frank Rich, writing an op-ed column in the *New York Times*, notes the great irony at work in the far-right bloggers, radio hosts, Glenn Beck, and Fox News's egging-on of the anti-mosque sentiment and overt attacks on Islam. He points out that those who were most in favor of the war were, by these actions, essentially undermining General Petraeus and the war strategy. How could America convince Muslims that ours was not a war against Islam and that we were only going to be successful if we won the "hearts and minds" of Muslims worldwide?[8]

For those accustomed to dividing everything in the world into easy and misleading binaries, the complexities of twenty-first-century global issues must be maddening. I would feel sorry for them if their words and actions weren't so damning to our country, to our Constitutional democracy, and to our place in the leadership of the world. It is hard to remain a silent witness to Islamophobic fear ginned up to fever pitch—the proposed cultural center called "a terrorist command center" by commentators and propagandists—and it was sadly laughable to see polls that, partially as a result, showed one-fifth of Americans believe that our president—who had openly defended our Constitutional guarantee of freedom of religion in response to it—was himself accused of being a "secret Muslim."[9] What dumb-asses, right? Right??? But name-calling is too cheap a response. Fun, yes, but it's ultimately not enough. I do not make my living as a comedian. I write and teach about communication and cultures. Somewhere between watchful silence and name-calling humor there emerges for me, and I hope for you, the felt need *to act*. To do something more meaningful and productive. To *say* something that matters.

So how should we talk to each other? What should we do? What language choices should we make that intelligently evoke our own sane, liberal anger without resorting to the tit-for-tat rhetorical strategy of setting off our own narrative IEDs?

Full disclosure: I am guilty of purposefully setting off one of those rhetorical explosions in the first few pages of the last chapter. In it, I referred more than a few times to our enemies on the far right as "dumb-asses." I used that term for two reasons. First, I used it because it perfectly captures my anger against those who would deny, say, evolution, or climate change; or who fail to support health care reform or public education; those who would alter textbooks and curricula on ideological grounds; or those who recruit the young for martyrdom; and so on. They *are* dumb-asses who are on the wrong side of empirical evidence, raw facts, science, and civilization. And second, I said it because it was fun, a little naughty, a little self-indulgent, a sign to my readers that understanding and using our anger does not mean giving up a sense of humor.

Try it yourself at home. Say aloud, "these f*&%ing people are dumb-asses!" Probably it will release some of that pent-up anger and resentment in your chest as well as bring a brief smile to your lips. *Dumb-asses.* Saying it *feels* good. Modifying it with "f*&%ing" makes it feel even better.

Ah, but therein lies the rub. Just because it feels good doesn't mean we should do it. According to the ordinary rules of polite conduct, by calling our enemies f*&%ing dumb-asses you and I fall into their corrosive trap. We become complicit in a mean world constructed out of binary opposites: us/them; right/left; true believers/infidels.[10]

As the Consortium for Strategic Communication[11] studies in counter-terrorism have shown, when the global war on terror is reduced to a battle of binary opposites, hatred deepens and recruitment to extremist groups flourishes. We play into their hands. For example, when some of our troops don, as they have done, arm patches that read "Pork-Eating Crusader" (in both English and

Arabic), it does absolutely nothing to promote cultural understanding, much less further dialogue with local populations. It divides them from those they are there to "free." It offers evidence—even if it isn't intended to—of our disrespect for Muslims and of our invasion and occupation of their lands and of our collective cultural stupidity about anything that isn't American.

By wearing these patches, our troops are daily planting narrative IEDs, spreading fear and reinforcing the political interests of the violent extremists by reinforcing *their* narrative: we are the Christian invaders, the occupiers, the armed force that disrupted their society and threatens to steal their oil and treasures—not too dissimilar to the Medieval Christian Crusaders. Those knights, too, were pork-eating Crusaders. Why, American soldier, would you wear the patch if you didn't identify with the comparison? Why, American leaders, would you tolerate this obvious insult to Islam if you did not intend to insult Islam? How can you repeatedly claim that this invasion is not a holy war against Muslims when you identify closely with those historical figures who did, in fact, wage a holy war against Muslims?

Pork-Eating Crusader. Another narrative IED. Worn proudly into battle it adds rhetorical power to an existing local narrative context, only deepening the doubt about our motives and mission. See how the narrative damage spreads? Moreover, from a strategic communication perspective, what legitimate purpose does it serve? What goal for our side is it likely to accomplish? The answer is: none. We have succeeded only in handing the enemy another narrative victory.

From a strategic communication perspective, the old linear model that places emphasis on the motives and meanings of a sender and the actual wording of a message ignores not only fifty years of communication research but also fails to recognize that interpretations of messages—of narratives—are local. Viewed this way, wearing the arm patch of a pork-eating Crusader is corrosive to civil discourse[12] because it is selfish in the strict sense of the term. It disrespects the Other and disregards the consequences of that disrespect. It is a joke that falls, literally, on deaf ears. Or worse, ears that have already been poisoned by the enemies' master narrative. It has a rhetorical afterlife that will live on far beyond its moment of expression.[13]

One solid lesson learned from twentieth century communication theories is captured in the image of a double helix, as explicated by Professor Frank E. X. Dance in 1967.[14] The image of a double helix reveals the concept of communication between people, groups, or nations, to be ongoing, irreversible, unrepeatable, and infinite. Once something is said, it cannot be "unsaid." Saying "I take it back" is an exercise in mindless futility because the damage is already done and because we have already moved beyond that utterance in time and space. Saying "I'm sorry" is not much of an improvement, although it can be helpful in repairing the damage if it is sincere.

I use this double helix image and description to underscore the idea that the rhetorical damage caused by calling someone a dumb-ass—even if it is true—or wearing an arm patch that contains the message "Pork-Eating Crusader" cannot be undone. Or at least not easily. It requires *forgiveness* on behalf of the Other, and there are many positive things that have to be in place in the relationship before forgiveness is much of a real option. And sometimes forgiveness is just not bloody likely. Imagine Osama bin Laden "forgiving" America for our perceived transgressions against Islam and very real invasion of Iraq and Afghanistan. Yeah, *right*. Or how about most Americans "forgiving" 9/11?

Binary opposites do not encourage, nor, in many cases, even *allow for* reconciliation. They divide the world into "Crusader" or "infi-del" and name as just plain *wrong* anyone or anything that opposes them. So too, then, does my use throughout this manuscript of the idea of our "enemies"—for I truly believe they are our enemies—work precisely from that same logic of binary opposition, of "us" versus "them." I don't even have to be specific. I can mention a few icons of Otherness in my world—Palin, Beck, Limbaugh, Bachmann, bin Laden—and you will fill in your own blanks, close up the narrative for me. Together, as speaker and listener, we collaborate to plant and to detonate our narrative IEDs.

In fact, in the above paragraph I did it again. I included bin Laden as the last name in a list of domestic violent extremists, and my bet is that unless you count yourself in the other camp, you probably smiled at the inference. And given what I've said so far, it's not so crazy. After all, al-Qaeda and the far right in America work off pretty much the same narrative script: the world is in chaos and disorder; we've fallen away from True Islam (or the True Constitution); what is needed is to reinstate the Caliphate (or Reagan Caliphate) and reinstitute the law (or Sharia); and to do this we must wage a political holy war (or jihad) against those who occupy our lands and who negatively influence our culture. Bin Laden calls for true believers to join his cause and to make themselves ready for martyrdom. Glenn Beck, et al., call for all true believers in the Constitution to join the Tea Party cause and make themselves ready for something very much like what Debra Medina calls "the tree of freedom [that] is occasionally watered with the blood of tyrants and patriots." Following this lead, is it any wonder that a conservative blogger calling himself Solly Forell called for the assassination of President Obama?[15]

Fear is what conservatives rely on to rally the votes. Fear of change. Fear of reform. Fear of a Black president. Fear of gay marriage. Fear of gays in the military. Fear of a woman's right to choose. Fear of government programs that *we elected* them to help create and responsibly manage. At the root all of their fear campaigns is a shrill overheated righteousness directed against anything or anyone who dares to disturb the status quo or who threatens to take away their guns, their prejudice, and/or their money. And for years, their program of fear coupled with shrill delivery has been quite effective. Paul Krugman, writing the morning after the health care victory in March, put it this way:

> The campaign of fear hasn't been carried out by a radical fringe, unconnected to the Republican establishment. On the contrary, that establishment has been involved and approving all the way. Politicians like Sarah Palin—who was, let us remember, the G.O.P.'s vice-presidential candidate—eagerly spread the death panel lie, and supposedly reasonable, moderate politicians like Senator Chuck Grassley refused to say that it was untrue. On the eve of the big vote, Republican members of Congress warned that "freedom dies a little bit today" and accused Democrats of

"totalitarian tactics," which I believe means the process known as "voting." ...

In the end, a vicious, unprincipled fear offensive failed to block reform. This time, fear struck out.[16]

Using fear to scare up votes is not new to American politics. But it reminds me of how far we have fallen from the ideal of appealing to "the common good" that defines the relationship of the individual to society in a democratic nation and was the basis for the very Constitution and Bill of Rights the right claims to protect. Many conservatives who wear the Republican stripe seem to have lost that sense entirely. Evidence: the health care reform bill was the first time in modern history that a major piece of legislation passed Congress without a single Republican vote.

But perhaps I should not be surprised. Our collective lack of empathy for the Other has moved the bar for everything else. Consider, if you will, this official government account of what constitutes torture for those accused of being our enemies:

> According to Justice Department memos released last year, the medical service opined that sleep deprivation up to 180 hours didn't qualify as torture. It determined that confinement in a dark, small space for 18 hours a day was acceptable. It said detainees could be exposed to cold air or hosed down with cold water for up to two-thirds of the time it takes for hypothermia to set in. And it advised that placing a detainee in handcuffs attached by a chain to a ceiling, then forcing him to stand with his feet shackled to a bolt in the floor, "does not result in significant pain for the subject." [17]

As anyone familiar with the horrors, as well as the debate over what happened at Guantanamo and Abu Ghraib, knows, the torture of so-called "enemy combatants" didn't stop there. Eleven detainees died at the hands of interrogators, some from asphyxiation with cloth stuffed down their throats, others suffocated with a plastic bag knotted around their head.[18] Dogs were used. Nudity. Sexual humiliation. Waterboarding.

The use of these "enhanced interrogation techniques," authorized by Secretary of Defense Donald Rumsfeld and given legal credence by

Attorney General Alberto Gonzalez as well as legal counsel John Yoo, essentially overturned in the world's mind the image of the United States as representing a higher standard, and largely reinforced the enemies' ability to successfully recruit new fighters to their cause. Although I am no great fan of Senator John McCain, his testimony in 2005 about the profound wrongness of such techniques deserves high praise:

> We are Americans. We hold ourselves to humane standards of treatment no matter how terribly evil they [enemy combatants] may be. To do otherwise undermines our security, and it also undermines our greatness as a nation. We are not simply another country. We stand for a lot more than that in the world, a moral mission, one of freedom and democracy and human rights at home and abroad.... The enemy we fight has no respect for human life or human rights. They don't deserve our sympathy. But this is not about who they are.... It is about who we are. Those are values that distinguish us from our enemies.[19]

Again: "It is about who we are. Those are values that distinguish us from our enemies." I think of these words a lot. I wonder, though, from the vantage afforded by five years time, the continuing war, a near disastrous financial meltdown, a year spent listening to the nonsense that passed as debate over health care reform, the launch of the Tea Bag Party, and a steady ratcheting up of the terrorist rhetoric on the far right, whether those of us on the left and center can hold to those values? Or whether we even should.

More and more I am persuaded to think differently about styles of argument as a result of drawing a parallel between strategic communication in the current battle of narratives and Alan Dershowitz's argument about the need to suspend the rules banning torture when there is a "ticking clock" and the likelihood of mass casualties.[20] At first this may seem like quite a stretch. After all, Dershowitz is talking about suspected terrorists who may know something about an impending attack on the United States.

Yet the analogy is useful. From where I sit nightly watching the news reports and following bloggers, the domestic enemies of the United States who are literally terrorizing us with their twisted narrative IEDs are, in fact, planning an attack on the government of our country. In fact, to listen to them, their campaign has already begun. Theirs, too, is a war of ideas and we, my friends, are the enemy. We are the Other.

Their mediated leaders, much like Osama bin Laden on videotape, reiterate the same basic narrative about the need to take back "their" country, and the more lunatic among them, including serving soldiers and officers in the U. S. military organized as "Oath Keepers," even go so far as to advocate stockpiling guns and ammunition against the day that President Obama declares a national emergency.[21] As Frank Rich, drawing from a report last year from the Southern Poverty Law Center observes:

> The unhinged and sometimes armed anti-government right that was thought to have vaporized after its Oklahoma apotheosis is making a comeback. And now it is finding common cause with some elements of the diverse, far-flung and still inchoate Tea Party movement. All it takes is a few self-styled "patriots" to sow havoc. [22]

Rich also mentions the murder-suicide of Andrew Joseph Stack, III, the tax protester who flew his plane into the IRS building in Austin, Texas, after leaving a fiery note that blamed the government and the tax code for his problems and echoed Tea Party rants. But what makes his case singular, Rich continues, is that

> that rant inspired like-minded Americans to create instant Facebook shrines to his martyrdom. Soon enough, some cowed politicians, including the newly minted Tea Party hero Scott Brown, were publicly empathizing with Stack's credo—rather than risk crossing the most unforgiving brigade in their base.

Representative Steve King, Republican of Iowa, even rationalized Stack's crime. "It's sad the incident in Texas happened," he said, "but by the same token, it's an agency that is unnecessary. And when the day comes when that is over and we abolish the

I.R.S., it's going to be a happy day for America." No one in King's caucus condemned these remarks.

Martyrdom sites? *Really*? Once again, the parallels between the ideological and narrative framework for the far enemy is more and more sounding familiar when adopted by the near enemy. So what is a liberal-minded, patriotic fellow who sees these actions as threatening the beautiful idea of America to do? How should I—by which I also include you—engage the near enemy? How should we fight this war of ideas?

Is it a good idea, a rational and sane idea, to suspend the rules of civic engagement that have defined those of us who identify with the left and center as being "better than that"? Is it a good idea to remain unwilling to allow our anger to deploy our own narrative IEDs in public places? Does it make good strategic communication sense to believe that if we sometimes behave badly we lose the moral battle—much less our country—because we lose polite debating points?

Finally: what do these questions say about smart and dumb uses of binary opposites, of narrative IEDs, and even of propaganda? And should we be willing to deploy these rhetorical tools to counter the binaries, the IEDs, the assaults on reason, and the outright propaganda used by their side to fight this war of ideas?

Make no mistake, our enemies (there's that binary opposition again) deploy all of them. Consider, for example, the following list of well-known propaganda techniques, first identified by the Institute for Propaganda Analysis in 1937:[23]

- Name calling
- Glittering generalities
- Euphemisms
- Transfer
- Testimonial
- Plain Folks
- Bandwagoning
- Fear

- Logical fallacy
- Unwarranted extrapolation

Now, just for fun, tune in to Fox News. Keep score with a pad and pencil of the number of propaganda techniques that are used by the commentators to provide "perspective," to forward "arguments" about "the way things are today" or "what we should do." For fun, I'll get you started.

- Name calling (seeks to make us form a judgment to reject and condemn without examining the evidence)

   Obama is a socialist; Hillary Clinton is a fascist; Liberals are weak

- Glittering generalities (seeks to make us approve and accept without examining the evidence)

   [Fill in a politician's name here] and then associate that name with Christianity, democracy, patriotism, motherhood, father-hood, science, medicine, health, and, of course, love

- Euphemisms

   "No Child Left Behind"; the "Patriot Act," which more fairly should have been labeled "Every Child Taught Only to Test, and Many of Them Badly" and "The Fear and Loathing of Others Act"

- Transfer (associating the virtues/vices of one thing with some-thing or someone else)

   Religion: *When a Republican or Tea Party member closes her or his speech with a public prayer, she or he is attempting to transfer religious prestige to the ideas being advocated.*

   Science: *Actors, pretending to be scientists and being paid by Big Pharma, in white lab coats tell us that "tests prove ..."*

   Medicine: *Medical doctors, now serving as U. S. Senators, explain why they favor a particular prescription for health care reform.*

   Terrorist: *During the health care reform protests, extremists created slogans and signs depicting the president as Osama bin Laden.*

- Testimonial

  Beauty queens, country music or rock stars, and celebrities are packaged with a political speech, candidate, or campaign

- Plain Folks

  Sarah Palin calls herself a "hockey mom" and appeals to "the real people in this country"

- Bandwagoning

  Mike Huckabee, Sarah Palin, etc. identifying with the Tea Party once it gained some media attention and popular support

- Fear

  Tea Party uses fear of big government, a Black president, and taxes; Republicans, Ann Coulter, and Fox News do much the same thing

- Logical fallacy

  Major Premise: *Barack Hussein Obama supports gun-control legislation.*

  Minor Premise: *All fascist regimes of the twentieth century have passed gun-control legislation.*

  Conclusion: *Barack Hussein Obama is a fascist.*

By now, as a liberal or even as a moderate, you are probably thinking—in the interest of a fair and balanced report, which is what we all claim to like to see—that we already have news analysts, comedians, and columnists doing this sort of propaganda work for us. And of course, we do: Keith Olbermann, Rachel Maddow, Jon Stewart, Stephen Colbert, Frank Rich, Paul Krugman, Andy Borowitz, etc. But regardless of how you feel disposed toward or against their views, they are media stars, not elected representatives. Nor are they ordinary citizens who have simply reached the political boiling point and who plan to do something about it. That, I hope, would be our job, our "word warrior" role in the war of ideas.

Yet we can learn from their examples. We can learn from their rhetorical management of their anger. Their skill at narrative. And more importantly, we can learn how they turn that anger into something far better, far more productive than "pork-eating Crusader" patches. For despite the obvious liberal bias in their reports and commentaries, these speakers from the left somehow generally maintain their cool and find interesting and even creative ways to channel their anger into talk or writing that makes a difference. Talk and writing that finds its way into social networks, blogs, and research articles. Talk that stirs the pot, lights fires, moves things along. Talk that effectively counters the domestic terrorist rhetoric and that lessens the likelihood of that domestic terrorist rhetoric going unchallenged. If they were academics relying on citation indices or impact ratings as the metric for evaluating the influence of their work, well, they would be superstars. And that is what this book is all about: *finding better ways to spread our narrative and counter theirs using all available means of persuasion.* Including smarter tactical deployments of binaries and narrative IEDs.

One clear strategy they all use is to employ *ridicule* and *humor* when discussing the dumb-asses. Sorry. Let me rephrase that last thought: One clear strategy is to employ ridicule and humor when discussing the views and actions of our enemies. Much better. For this reason I applaud the anti-Tea Party protesters at the University of Wisconsin, who, on April 15, 2010, infiltrated a Tea Party Tax Day demonstration with signs proclaiming "This is a Sign"; "I Love Puppies"; "Do You Need a Hug?"; and "Under 26, We've Got You Covered!" Similarly, the organization "The Other 95%" turned out with huge banners to remind the cameras that under President Obama, 95 percent of Americans pay less tax than we did under Bush. Or for that matter, under *every other administration* since Reagan!

Peter Beinart, blogging for the *Daily Beast*, also deploys humor and ridicule to counter the Tea Party. Following a study that showed Tea Party members to be older, wealthier, and more educated than the average American, he posted this comment: "What kind of adjective suits older, grumpy, well-off Americans who believe Democrats are communists, the poor have it too easy and white people are oppressed? The term 'Republican' comes to mind."[24]

Nor is this counter-narrative tactic unique to the United States. J.K. Rowling, best-selling author of the Harry Potter series, successfully dubbed the Conservative Party in the U.K. "the nasty party," for their renewed stance against using taxes to help single mothers. She tells her story:

> Women like me (for it is a curious fact that lone male parents are generally portrayed as heroes, whereas women left holding the baby are vilified) were, according to popular myth, a prime cause of social breakdown, and in it for all we could get: free money, state-funded accommodation, an easy life.
>
> An easy life. Between 1993 and 1997 I did the job of two parents, qualified and then worked as a secondary school teacher, wrote one and a half novels and did the planning for a further five. For a while, I was clinically depressed. To be told, over and over again, that I was feckless, lazy—even immoral—did not help.[25]

There is nothing funny about Rowling's story, but the ridicule in it combined with the humiliating label "the nasty party" had what Malcolm Gladwell calls a certain "stickiness" to it. But it also does other political work: it contributes to a division among Conservative women based on gender and based on family status. And, given the credibility of its source, the slogan and its political work were impossible to repress.

Interestingly, a research study by counter-terrorism expert J. Michael Waller entitled *Fighting the War of Ideas Like a Real War* reaches a similar tactical conclusion about the use of ridicule and humiliation. He observes that our "secret weapon worse than death" against radical extremists is precisely those strategic communication tactics, something Osama bin Laden says is worse than death at the hands of Americans.[26] Ridicule, especially when combined with humiliation, works because:

- It sticks;
- The target can't refute it;
- It is almost impossible to repress;
- It spreads on its own and multiplies with each re-telling;
- It boosts morale at home;

- Our enemy shows far greater intolerance to ridicule than we;

- Ridicule divides the enemy, damages its morale, and makes it less attractive to supporters and prospective recruits; and

- The ridicule-armed warrior need not fix a physical sight on the target. Ridicule will find its own way to the targeted individual. To the enemy, being ridiculed means losing respect. It means losing influence. It means losing followers and repelling potential new backers.

Kristin Fleischer also believes that humor and ridicule provide opportunities to counter terrorists.[27] From Umar Farouk Abdulmutallab, the Christmas Bomber of 2009 who was dubbed "the underwear bomber," to Special Forces accounts of using name-calling and ridicule to tease Taliban fighters into giving away their positions, to comedian Jeff Dunham's use of the "Achmed the Dead Terrorist" suicide bomber dummy, there are clear advantages to the deployment of this strategy against—and about—extremists.

Think of any recent political scandal on either side of the aisle: Larry Craig's "wide stance" defense; John Edwards's "baby daddy" debacle; Mark Sanford's "soul mate" confession; Rod Blagojevich's attempted sale of Obama's Senate seat; John Ensign's affair with an aide who is the wife of a former aide; and so on. My point is that while it is entirely reasonable to respond to each of these persons and events as human tragedies—tragedies of judgment—our commentators chose to respond to them as comedies. As farce. As sources for ridicule, humiliation, and humor. As, well, *dumb-asses*.

Kenneth Burke teaches us that when confronted with conflict we choose between framing it as a comedy or as a tragedy. He further opines that only comedy offers hope. Think of it this way: the deployment of binaries and narrative IEDs in the service of hope may be a good thing. It offers what Burke calls "perspective by incongruity." It is—pardon me for this one, Burke fans—a "counter-statement."[28] All in all what we have is a way of countering extremist narratives that does not require us to get very dirty, nor does it reduce us to wearing pork-eating Crusader arm patches. What it does require is a sense of humor and a perspective on the uses of humor and ridicule *to influence how what is being said should be seen and understood.*

But that is not all we must do. Laughter is but one tool in the Battle of Narrative Handbook. It is an IED, one way of complicating the binary, exposing inauthenticity and deception, pointing out lies. I am generally content to let our media stars, the comedians and pundits, do the heavy lifting—that is, after all, their job—and to reserve for myself only an occasional expletive. And then, delivered only with a big smile.

But no matter who is responsible for deploying them, we cannot win this war of ideas with IEDs alone. We cannot afford to rely on "message bombs" to do the work that must be done. We have other ways of reaching those who might yet be persuaded, as well as those who might yet listen to reason. We have a core narrative to re-articulate. We have values to defend. And we have networks and communities to involve. That's why there are further chapters to be read and circulated. If you are still with me, please press on. As Robert Frost might have put it, "We have miles to go before we rest."

I began this chapter with a call to embrace the good and the evil in our hearts. To come to terms with the duality of our own narratives. And in so doing, to purify ourselves before taking up this fight by owning the anger, the frustration, the impulse we sometimes feel to strike out against the violent extremists near and far. Along the way I have asked some hard questions about the role of free speech and civil discourse, and I have implied that continuing along this rhetorical path as we have has only brought us to the brink of losing that beautiful idea that is America, the strength it offers each of us and the narrative of hope that it offers to the world.

At the very beginning of this quest I said this would be dangerous work. And it will be. It is dangerous to purify your own narrative, and it is dangerous to emerge on the other side of that process armed with new knowledge about the struggle between good and evil that defines who we are, who we can be, to ourselves, and that uses that narrative power to define ourselves to the world. To engage in the work we were made to do. That we must do if America is to survive.

We must learn from our enemies as well as from friends. Our enemies have learned that their core narrative is dedicated to the singular idea of preserving binary opposites and treating every day as another narrative IED opportunity. Failing that, they just say "no." We must use their lack of knowledge and their simpleminded tactics against them. We must find new ways to transcend binaries while at the same time making use of them when it is productive to do so. And we must acquire not only the capability, the network technologies, to not be surprised but to clearly anticipate their IEDs and to meet them, and to expose them, with our own array of counter measures.

Buddha is a laughing god. We must also learn from his example.

3. Birthers, Social Justice & the Texas Textbook Massacre

The Nature of Paranoid Style, Conspiracies, and the Ruse Narrative in Extremist Discourse

In our studies of extremist narratives it has been helpful to make pragmatic use of Kenneth Burke's theory of form. Burke teaches us to think about stories in the old fashioned modernist way, essentially derived from Aristotle (all stories have beginnings, middles, and endings) but improved through applications of a Jungian sensitivity to archetypes and the psychology of persuasive appeals that rely on the satisfaction of desired outcomes rooted in binary conflicts: good versus evil, believers versus infidels, us versus them.

From Burke we learn to appreciate the overarching trajectory of narratives, literally a movement from beginnings to preferred endings, as well as the peculiar power vested in the urgent human need for completion, for resolution, for final victory, for "happy endings." Hence, as Burke puts it, "form *is* the appeal."[1] Viewed neutrally, Burke's philosophy of form affords a way of thinking about narratives as holistic organizing devices aimed at satisfying a particular purpose or end. When read alongside the moral philosopher Alasdair MacIntyre's statement, "I can only answer the question 'What am I to do?' if I can answer the prior question 'Of what story or stories do I find myself a part?',"[2] we see not only the way the world is put together in words but also how we find our place in it.

In fact, understanding how narratives matter allows us to answer four pivotal questions:

1. How do we make sense of the events of everyday life?

2. How do we connect new information to existing patterns of meaning, or reconcile contradictory information to those patterns of meaning?

3. How do we justify our resulting actions?

4. How do we explain where we want to be in the future and what we are working toward?

So it is that we explain the world to ourselves and others. So it is, too, that we find work in it to do.

Viewed not so neutrally, Burke's ideas about form, MacIntyre's recognition of the centrality of narrative form to identity, and the four questions we answer with recourse to our narratives reveal a darker side of extremist narrative reasoning: *the conspiracy narrative.*

Conspiracies involve a narrative construction of the world in which binary oppositions are defined by a righteous conflict pitting a true believer against a *trickster* only posing as One Of Us or One Who Can Be Trusted. The trickster may be a person (e.g., Obama) or a group (e.g., the Jews, Liberals, Democrats). The primary motivation for combating the trickster is to make right the world again, but the method for accomplishing that end is the perpetration of *fear.* As a particular kind of narrative, the trickster trajectory may only be resolved by either *heroic effort* or *noble sacrifice.* There is no such thing as détente. Nor is appeasement an answer. This is a narrative *war*, baby. They are out to get us, make no mistake.

I am also interested in applying Richard Hofstadter's notion of "The Paranoid Style in American Politics" to these extremist conspiracy narratives. Hofstadter begins his famous essay with this observation:

American politics has often been an arena for angry minds. In recent years we have seen angry minds at work mainly among extreme right-wingers, who have now demonstrated in the Goldwater movement how much political leverage can be got out of the animosities and passions of a small minority. But behind this I believe there is a style of mind that is far from new and that is not necessarily right-wing. I call it the paranoid style simply because no other word adequately evokes the sense of heated exaggeration, suspiciousness, and conspiratorial fantasy that I have in mind.[3]

Burke's conception of form when combined with Hoftstadter's notion of "the paranoid style" is useful when examining extremist conspiracy discourse because when read together they encourage a closer look at specific, recurring conspiracy narratives that, for extremist audiences, do in fact "hang together" and "ring true."

It also allows us to understand how listeners and readers organize a paranoid worldview rooted in a particular "master narrative"—often an "origins tale" that is a commingling of religion and politics—and that is threatened by a conspiracy aimed at destroying it. As a revealed narrative, the threat to what we believe (*our* master narrative) and to what we value (*our* way of life) does the work of gaining close identification not only with the supposed "truth" of the conspiracy account. But moreover, that close identification has clear implications about what needs to be done. No retreat. No surrender.

As Hofstadter points out: "The paranoid spokesman sees the fate of conspiracy in apocalyptic terms—he traffics in the birth and death of whole worlds, whole political orders, whole systems of human values. He is always manning the barricades of civilization. He constantly lives at a turning point."[4]

Given the critical mass of alleged right-wing conspiracies and their "stickiness factor," we may rephrase Hofstadter's "turning point" into what Malcolm Gladwell calls "the tipping point."[5]

In this chapter I want to use what I've learned about extremist master narratives and about conspiracies and the "paranoid style" to examine three contemporary issues that reveal an organized conspiracy worldview by the American far right: the Birther controversy over President Obama's nationality and ties to Islam; the "social justice is not what Jesus intended" rhetoric of Glenn Beck and others opposed to any perceived "redistribution of wealth"; and the successful attempt by ten dumb-ass and paranoid members of a Texas school board to rewrite American history based on an ultraconservative and Christian political agenda. As you will see, all three of these conspiracy narratives bear a curious relationship to like extremist conspiracy narratives in the extremist Muslim world.

Birthers[6] contend that Barack Obama was not born in the United States, but in Kenya, and that his Hawaiian birth certificate is a forgery perpetrated by liberal/Muslim conspirators to keep his "true faith" secret. Birthers also espouse the notion that Obama did not take the oath of office on a Bible, but instead on the Qur'an.[7] Claims of Obama's secret Muslim identity and other nefarious plots have been circulated by numerous sources in the United States (e.g., Fox News), including several spurious e-mail messages that claim he was educated in a radical Wahabi school. One such e-mail stated the following:

> Lolo Soetoro, the second husband of Obama's mother, Ann Dunham, introduced his stepson to Islam. Obama was enrolled in a Wahabi [sic] school in Jakarta. Wahabism [sic] is the RADICAL teaching that is followed by the Muslim terrorists who are now waging Jihad against the western world. ... The Muslims have said they plan on destroying the U.S. from the inside out, what better way to start than at the highest level through the President of the United States, one of their own!!!![8]

David Gaubatz, an anti-Islam activist with ties to numerous U.S. Congressmen, wrote at the time of Obama's election that "a vote for Hussein [sic] Obama is a vote for Sharia law."[9] Ironically, Fred Phelps, the "minister" of the radical fundamentalist Westboro Baptist Church and leader of sick protests against homosexuals at the funerals of soldiers, and at the site of community grieving over dead coal miners, advocates pretty much the same law for America, yet few on the right have stepped up to decry either his message or his means.[10]

Since Obama's election Birthers have extended the range of their paranoid fantasies to attack Attorney General Eric Holder's position—based on a conservative Supreme Court decision—to allow enemy combatants held in captivity to have legal counsel. Birthers and other ultraconservatives see this move as another sign of Obama's desire to free, or at least give aid and comfort to, Muslim extremists. Liz Cheney called the lawyers who agreed to defend prisoners at Guantanamo the "al Qaeda 7," not only questioning their loyalty but, in a move clearly reminiscent of Joseph McCarthy during the cold war, also questioning their political views, asking, unambiguously, "what values do they share?"[11]

It is worth noting that a number of conservatives, including Kenneth Starr and Lindsey Graham, immediately spoke out against Liz Cheney, reminding citizens that not only is it true that our Constitution guarantees the right of counsel but moreover that questioning the integrity of lawyers on nothing more solid than their willingness to uphold that Constitutional guarantee was in poor taste.[12] Cheney, of course, did not back down. On her Keep America Safe website (http://www.keepamericasafe.com/) a steady stream of fear-based attacks against the lawyers, Obama, and Holder continued, proving, if nothing else, that she is her father's daughter and a seasoned conspiracy propagandist.[13]

Her media strategy is not surprising. At least since the age of McCarthy, no propagandist on the far right ever backs down or admits she or he is wrong, even when presented with the facts and even when those facts come from those in their own camp. They just keep repeating the false charges, continue to attach the same negative labels to their opponents, and ratchet up the fear mongering and conspiracy rhetoric. Yesterday's McCarthyism—labeling his political opponents as "Communists"—spawned today's allegations of Obama being a "Socialist" and his programs as "Socialism," with neither term in either era ever being clearly defined. You would think Americans would learn from the past, but we do not.

That we don't learn propaganda lessons from the past is not entirely surprising. When it comes to the use of fear and innuendo to influence publics, psychology trumps history. The German propaganda minister Joseph Goebbels taught by example today's users how to sell "the big lie," while the American father of public relations and advertising, Edward Bernays, taught them the art of appealing to what he called "the group mind" in order to "engineer consent."[14] Today, these extremely effective psychological techniques for spreading fear are well documented by scholars and used to maximum effect by a wide variety of practitioners, from advertisers and marketing firms to political organizations to the military in "PSYOPS" operations.[15]

One lesson for educators: we need to teach propaganda theory and critical approaches to combating it in our classes. Lesson for community organizers: you need to hold seminars on propaganda techniques and use local examples to document your case. Lesson for everyone: just because propaganda sounds like old news doesn't mean it can't be useful.

But there is more going on within conspiracy propaganda than the psychology of fear. For those of us who study extremist narratives, there is a striking resemblance in tone, content, and form between the Birthers/Cheney storyline and the master narrative story form known as "the ruse" adopted by the Islamists about the abolition of the Ottoman Caliphate in 1924 by the president of the Turkish Republic, Mustafa Kemal Atatürk. According to Islamists, Ataturk was part of a sinister conspiracy against Islam and was, himself, a secret Jew (apparently a member of the Dönme sect) working on behalf of global Zionism to eliminate Islam. His widespread adoption of a Western style of dress and his transfer from Sharia to a secular laws structure was further proof of his true identity and his intent to corrupt Muslim values and way of life.[16]

For scholars interested in narratives, this is an example of "the ruse story," a favorite story form among conspiracy theorists. It begins with an imagined conflict between a trickster, who only pretends the true faith or loyalty, and a true believer or loyal citizen who recognizes the deceit. The storyline unfolds as a series of allegations that link current events to the original ruse, reaching a climax when the hoped for revelation of the trickster's true identity and purpose is finally accomplished.

It is worth noting also that once the ruse story form is put into play, there is no way to resolve the conflict other than in the preferred revelation of deceit. In other words, just because you are, in fact, paranoid, doesn't mean that someone isn't out to deceive you. That this trickster can continue to deceive is only given added warrant by the fact that he/she has not yet been caught and her/his true identity and purpose have not yet been revealed. In other words, once in a conspiracy narrative, always in a conspiracy narrative. The truth *will not* set you free.

For the Birthers, President Obama *will always be* an illegal alien posing as a native born son. Unless or until he is eliminated from office and/or exposed as a fraud. But that is not the end of it. Because conspiracy narratives always connect new events to the existing paranoid worldview and storyline, Obama's role as a trickster extends to his alleged attempt to make America a socialist nation. It doesn't matter if the issue is health care reform, judicial nominations, gay marriage, financial sector reform, gun control, immigration policy, terrorism, the tragic oil leak in the Gulf, or education, for those on the far right who are prone to conspiracy theories, having a perceived trickster in the White House is cause enough to connect him and the larger conspiracy to every dot that doesn't fit neatly into their worldview.

Which brings me to that well-known Communist and Nazi idea: social justice.

Social justice[17] seems to be a truly odd concept to become the basis for another conspiracy theory from the far right, but thanks to Glenn Beck and his supporters in the blogosphere, it has become exactly that: "I beg you, look for the words 'social justice' or 'economic justice' on your church web site. ... If you find it, run as fast as you can. Social justice and economic justice, they are code words. Now, am I advising people to leave their church? Yes!"[18]

Despite the outcry from many church leaders, Beck did not back down. In a second broadcast aired on March 11, 2010, "Beck returned to the subject, insisting that the notion of social justice is 'a perversion of the Gospel,' and 'not what Jesus would say.' He wasn't kidding. He went on to say that Americans should be skeptical of religious leaders who are 'basing their religion on social justice,' and explained his fear that concern for social justice is a problem 'infecting all' faith traditions."[19]

Beck likened social justice to both Naziism and Communism on the grounds that social justice is "a code word" for the redistribution of wealth. In fact, Beck's views echo those of philosopher Friedrich Hayek, who was famous for his lifelong opposition to the term on the grounds that it lacked a common definition and that it was invoked as a way to legislate and regulate order and power. In essence, Hayek's objections were also economic as well as philosophical; he deplored the use of the idea to promote "a living wage" and to create programs to lessen unemployment.

Church leaders fired back, including leaders from Beck's own Mormon Church, and the Reverend Jim Wallis (a Christian evangelical and CEO of Sojourners), and Reverend Canon Peg Chemberlin, president of the National Council of Churches of Christ USA (representing over one hundred churches and forty-five million members). Reverend Chemberlin put it this way:

> I hesitated to respond, because it seemed like such a ridiculous statement. But this is really an attack ... a misunderstanding, at least, of what the Bible says. Justice is a concept throughout the scriptures. It's one that should be and must be organized around any congregation.... It's very disturbing. He's speaking on behalf of his political views and trying to take out of the biblical text the things that are going to oppose his political views. This is primarily a political motivation.... It's not that Christians haven't been Nazis and socialists, but we're not talking about political parties here. We're talking about 2,000-year-old gospel.[20]

Beck's seemingly mindless association of a long held religious tradition with Naziism and Communism is actually easily explained. What Beck is really attacking is the perceived liberal conspiracy to redistribute wealth. In his worldview, "social justice" is just a code word for any attempt by government to raise taxes, legislate equality and promote equity, or to provide economic protection for the poor. Churches who engage in these "liberal" activities are unwitting co-conspirators in the vast leftist plot to take over the world.

Stop laughing. He means it. This man/clown is seriously paranoid. Dr. Michael Bader, in an article published in *Psychology Today* called "We Need to Have Empathy for the Tea Partiers," defines Beck's pathology this way:

> The paranoid strategy is to generate a narrative that finally "explains it all." A narrative—a set of beliefs about the way the world is and is supposed to be—helps make sense of chaos. It reduces guilt and self-blame by projecting it onto someone else. And it restores a sense of agency by offering up an enemy to fight. Finally, it offers hope that if "they"—the enemy, the

conspirators—can be avoided or destroyed, the paranoid person's core feelings of helplessness and devaluation will go away.[21]

The idea that Beck the paranoid must generate a narrative that "explains it all" is key. But the cause of his paranoia—feelings of helplessness and devaluation—might not seem to fit. After all, Beck is successful: he is a New York Times number one best-selling author, the CEO of his own media firm, quite wealthy, and, as of this writing, one of the most popular commentators on the air. He is a Rupert Murdoch-style capitalist who profits by fanning the flames of political contention. He is simply following the cardinal rule of the tabloid journalist: if people believe it, it must be true! Or as communication scholar Paul Watzlawick rephrases the Chicago School sociologist W.I. Thomas: "What is real is what people treat as real."[22]

Despite his current success, Beck's childhood was riddled with painful themes that often surface in the personal narratives of the paranoid: an unhappy home life, the divorce of his parents, the suicide of his alcoholic mother and later also his stepbrother, and a well-spun drug and alcohol aimlessness that defined his youth and young adulthood. His first marriage ended, despite producing two children. Yet this once down and out self-professed failure found his new life by following his own twelve-step program that began with his conversion to the Mormon Church, giving his life to God, and finding a new soulmate. Two more children, and a big house in Connecticut. Good for Glenn! Always glad to see a person turn around a sad childhood and misspent youth.

But as with Beck, the true paranoid seldom feels their success is fully deserved. Nor is success likely to last. After all, there is a vast network of conspiring Others who threaten the narrative upon which the paranoid has built a life. What is needed is constant reinforcement of that narrative and a surround of people who see the world as you do and who buy your story. What better way to accomplish that reinforcement and narrative surround than by using mass communication to reach others who think and feel as you do, and who are similarly frightened people? Glenn Beck is not the first person to realize his vision through the power of speech delivered over the airwaves. Arrogance, anger, and self-righteousness now pass for personal therapy. Fear is the weapon of mass persuasion he unleashes on the naïve and disenfranchised of the world. Then, because they choose to believe him instead of in Obama's programs designed to actually help them, they become complicit in their own oppression.[23]

Fear is the drug of choice for the paranoid. This is because paranoia works best when you infect others with your fears. So is it any wonder that this is the man no less an organization than the Anti-Defamation League has called "fearmonger-in-chief"[24] and that *Time* magazine characterized as a spokesperson who views America as constantly "under siege."[25] No. Beck's extremist[26] narrative vision for the future of our country is firmly rooted in fear mingled with nostalgia for a Founding Fathers mythic past that is given emotional warrant by his oft-repeated and teary-eyed claim that "I love my country." It is a superb performance of the paranoid self, all jacked up on conspiracy as the drug of choice.

Which in turn, is all wrapped up in dollar signs. Perhaps it is all about the Benjamins. Beginning in late April 2010, Beck, chastened perhaps by religious leaders for his stance against social justice, initiated a monologue about God speaking directly to him, telling him His plan. As absurd as this appeal to authority to counteract mere human criticism may seem, it carries with it a financial agenda. As political blogger Bob Cesca puts it: "The overarching theme of this monologue is that God is speaking directly to Glenn Beck and giving him the plan. It's classic televangelism, which is commonly seen as nothing more than an exploitation of religious naiveté with the goal of making the televangelist rich."[27]

Given that agenda, and while it may seem irrational given his professed Mormon faith and professed Christian values, to take on the idea of social justice is not really so odd after all. For what drives this narrative of liberal conspiracy he perceives to threaten him is less a matter of God than of Mammon. It's all about the money. It's all about him being able to "de-code" the language of the enemy, to read into the words "social justice" *a redistribution of wealth* and to find in the ideas of equality and equity under the law the true face of ideological evil. This is what the dollarless Communists did. This is what the National Socialists (aka Nazis) did when they seized the assets of Jews. For Beck, it doesn't matter that National Socialism and Communism aren't the same thing. It's all part of the same economic and political narrative fabric sewn together with gold threads.

Keep your social justice hands off the money! And while you are at it, lower my taxes. Rescind social policies and institutions designed to help the poor. Are there not poor houses? Scrooge, before his awakening to the good of social justice, was the perfect role model for Glenn Beck and the far right ultraconservatives.

Interestingly, this attack on the idea of social justice as the "wrongly understood" redistribution of (unearned) wealth is not new to conservative thought. For example, Michael Novak of the conservative American Enterprise Institute and a champion of Friedrich Hayek's ideas about social justice, offers this "rightly understood" approach:

> First, the skills it requires are those of inspiring, working with, and organizing others to accomplish together a work of justice. These are the elementary skills of civil society, through which free citizens exercise self–government by doing for themselves (that is, without turning to government) what needs to be done.
>
> The second characteristic ... is that it aims at the good of the city, not at the good of one agent only. Citizens may band together, as in pioneer days, to put up a school or build a bridge. They may get together in the modern city to hold a bake sale for some charitable cause, to repair a playground, to clean up the environment.[28]

What is missing from this formulation is any mention of empathy for the Other. Any accommodation for real poverty, real injustice, real disease. What we do have is a narrative about well-intentioned people with time on their hands joining together to purchase building supplies and spending a weekend or two in the company of like-minded others building bridges and schools, or holding bake sales.

How polite and easy. How civil. How white. Also, how lacking in conceptual depth, or strength of liberating purpose. For at its very core, social justice is not just about "free-thinking give-back" but is instead about using the great engines of government and faith to, as the Constitution puts it, "promote the common welfare." It is the very face we show to a common humanity and to our rightful obligation to see, as the Bible puts it, that "there but for the Grace of God, go I."

Historian Tony Judt worried that we don't see or feel that way as a nation anymore.[29] We used to. During the 1960s a Democratic-led Congress sponsored programs that the extremists today would gladly dismantle: "food stamps, Medicare, the Civil Rights Act, Medicaid, Head Start, the National Endowment for the Humanities, the National Endowment for the Arts and the Corporation for Public Broadcasting." And why is that?

According to Judt, we have been brainwashed into believing that "the public good" is not worth the bother. We've tuned out because of the toxic discourse "elevated to a cult by Know Nothings, States' Rightists, anti-tax campaigners and — most recently — the radio talk show demagogues of the Republican Right."

Ever since Reagan and the campaign against "big government" and for a sobering rhetoric of "no taxes," an absurd number of American citizens have been railroaded into believing that "a contribution to the provision of collective goods that individuals could never afford in isolation (roads, fire fighters, police, schools, lamp posts, post offices, not to mention soldiers, warships, and weapons) is rarely considered." It is the far right's narrative, they are sticking to it, and that it doesn't even make common sense or that the services they hope to dismantle are services that the right uses and takes advantage of on a daily basis is not relevant to their purposes.

Which doesn't mean the Reagan Revolution hasn't happened or that this Know-Nothing narrative isn't widely believed. Because it has and it is. If the last generation—the boomers—is lost to the cause of social justice, which Judt believes is true, then the next battleground for narrative is future generations.

And there is nowhere better to begin that campaign than with textbooks.

The Texas Textbook Massacre was announced in the *New York Times* with the following brief introduction:

The New York Times

March 12, 2010

Texas Conservatives Win Curriculum Change

By James C. McKinley, Jr.

AUSTIN, Tex. — After three days of turbulent meetings, the Texas Board of Education on Friday approved a social studies curriculum that will put a conservative stamp on history and economics textbooks, stressing the superiority of American capitalism, questioning the Founding Fathers' commitment to a purely secular government and presenting Republican political philosophies in a more positive light.

The vote was 10 to 5 along party lines, with all the Republicans on the board voting for it.

Some of the specifics of the proposed changes include:[30]

1. Delete Thomas Jefferson and replace his Enlightenment thinking with religious icon John Calvin. (Reason: Jefferson is responsible for the separation of church and state.)

2. Teachers are required to underscore the Judeo-Christian influences on the founding fathers. (Reason: to suggest, none too subtly, that we are primarily a Christian nation.)

3. Describe "U. S. government as a 'constitutional republic,' rather than 'democratic.'" (Reason: power. A "republic" is governed by charter—for example, the Constitution and Bill of Rights—whereas a "democracy" is governed by majority vote.)

4. Remove hip-hop as an "example of a significant cultural movement." (Reason: too much emphasis on minorities.)

5. No longer require that teachers provide instruction on why the U. S. Constitution does not promote a particular religion. (Reason: see items 1 and 2 above.)

6. When teaching McCarthyism, include "how the later release of the Venona papers confirmed suspicions of communist infiltration in U.S. government." When teaching Martin Luther King, Jr., also teach the negative impact of the Black Panthers. (Reason: to avoid criticism of conservatives and to avoid promoting ideas that were opposed by them.)

7. Provide substantive instruction in "the conservative resurgence of the 1980s and 1990s, including Phyllis Schlafly, the Contract with America, the Heritage Foundation, the Moral Majority and the National Rifle Association." (Reason: these people and organizations supported conservative causes.)

8. Ban teaching sex and gender differences. (Reason: to avoid discussions of homosexuality, transvestites, transsexuals, and what board member Barbara Cargill called "who knows what else.")

9. Replace most mentions of "capitalism" with "free enterprise." (Reason: according to board member Ken Mercer, it avoids the "negative connotation" of "capitalism.")

10. No longer require history teachers or textbooks to provide information about Senator Edward Kennedy or Supreme Court Justice Sonia Sotomayor. Encourage more coverage of President Ronald Reagan. (Reason: de-emphasize liberals and Democrats; underscore conservatives and Republicans.)

11. Omit Tejanos from list of "fallen heroes of the Alamo." (Reason: racism, maybe?)

Laurie Fendrich, writing for the *Chronicle of Higher Education*, likened the proposed curriculum changes to state propaganda:

The perversion of knowledge into state propaganda resembles nothing so much as what the Communist bloc did to ideas in the mid-20th century. More fearful of ideas than guns, they simply banned any ideas they didn't like. In wiping out Jefferson, in particular, the Texas board looks a lot like the communists who used to airbrush out of official state photos those who had been executed after the famous Czech show trials early in the 1950s.[31]

It is worth noting that no historians, economists, or sociologists were consulted about these issues, and that the Texas board was clear about its intentions to rewrite history from a conservative Christian ideological perspective. Don McLeroy, the leader of the conservative majority, put it this way: "History has already been skewed. Academia is skewed too far to the left."[32]

Ah, there it is. The monstrous head of our vast liberal conspiracy narrative rears itself once again.

One might say in response that just because those of us on the left have truth on our side doesn't make us wrong. We actually have read history, economics, and sociology and understand full well that Jefferson not only wrote the Constitution drawing heavily upon Enlightenment ideas, but also that he purposefully placed into it the "separation of church and state" to prevent the adoption of a state religion *as well as* to prevent the elevation of Christianity above all religions.

John Calvin, by contrast, was a man who wrote, in his *Institutes of the Christian Religion* (1559), that *the state must obey the dictates of the church*, and that a "consistory" made up of senior church members would be responsible for trying moral and religious offenses. A summary of Calvinism includes the following tenets:

> Man, who is corrupt, is confronted by the omnipotent (all powerful) and omnipresent (present everywhere) God who before the world began predestined some for eternal salvation (the Elect) while the others would suffer everlasting damnation (the Reprobates).
>
> The chosen few were saved by the operation of divine grace which cannot be challenged and cannot be earned by Man's merits. You might have led what you might have considered a perfectly good life that was true to God, but if you were a reprobate you remained one because for all your qualities you were inherently corrupt and God would know this even if you did not. However, a reprobate by behaving decently could achieve an inner conviction of salvation. An Elect could never fall from grace.

However, God remained the judge and lawgiver of men. Predestination remained a vital belief in Calvinism.[33]

Do these tenets of Calvin sound like the ideas that influenced the words found in our *Constitution of the United States*? To your way of thinking, would John Calvin's strict theology be an adequate replacement for Thomas Jefferson's Enlightenment influences? What is at stake here is truth, plain and simple.

And the minds of our children.

I would be remiss if I did not also mention that McLeroy and his conservative Christian cronies on the Texas school board have been diligently attempting to gain passage of language that would call into question biological and chemical evolution.[34] Long a proponent of the "strengths and weaknesses" clause to be attached to the teaching of evolution, McLeroy, a "Young Earth Creationist," has not yet been successful due, in part, to the public outrage among scientists in the state of Texas. Similar measures based on the same "strengths and weaknesses" language have appeared in Missouri and California but have not passed in the legislatures. This debate would be laughable if it were not so important to the future of science education. But it does remind me of the remark made by the wife of the bishop of Worcester following the publication of Darwin's *Origin of Species*: "Descended from monkeys? Let us hope that it is not true. But if it is true, let's hope it not become widely known."[35]

Only a true dumb-ass denies evolution. It is not "just a theory"; it is a theory *and* a fact. "Young Earth Creationism," on the other hand, is either fantasy or bad science fiction. As one of my colleagues put it, "It's as if these people believe that 'The Flintstones' is reality TV." Yet this spurious controversy continues despite overwhelming scientific evidence to the contrary. Why? The paranoid remains paranoid, clinging desperately to an old story, a mythology, of creation. It is the master narrative of Christian extremists who believe in a literal interpretation of the *Holy Bible*, regardless of its many translations, historically documented edits, and purposeful omissions made by men for political gain.

One more insult to our intelligence: part of the new rules for educators in Texas includes this ludicrous principle—that only the "positive aspects" of slavery be covered in history classes. And what might they be? I cannot imagine. But the dumb-ass nature of this plan is reminiscent of the confluence of fundamentalist Christian nonsense with a complete misunderstanding of history, as exemplified by this well-known (in Texas) comment by a former governor, Ma Ferguson. When asked what she thought of bi-lingual education, she replied: "If English was good enough for Jesus Christ, it's good enough for Texas."[36]

Connect the dots. The literal interpretation of the Bible, the literal interpretation of the Constitution, the literal interpretation of this, that, and the other thing. "Literal interpretation" is the enemy's Hammer of the Gods, and yet the two words spoken together constitute an oxymoron: *a figure of speech that combines normally contradictory terms.* If it is "literal," it doesn't admit to interpretation; if it is an "interpretation," it cannot be literal. It is an oxymoron for morons...IED intended.

Let's agree with Constitutional law professor Jamie Raskin, when, on March 1, 2006, in testimony before the U.S. Senate, he rightly observed: "People place their hand on the Bible and swear to uphold the Constitution. They don't put their hand on the Constitution and swear to uphold the Bible."[37]

If these ideological changes posing as curricular reform were limited to ensuring that only Texas students would be exposed to them, that would be bad for Texas. It would ensure that the sons and daughters of that stubbornly Republican state wouldn't be schooled in concepts, persons, facts, or events that are tested on standardized college entrance exams. But because the Texas decisions influence decision-making about textbook selections *across the country*, what may seem—very generously considered—like an honest ideological disagreement among Know-Nothing citizens on a state school board acquires the defining character of an ideological narrative gone wild.

What we have seen across extremist narratives is the powerful and essential idea of a vast liberal conspiracy that threatens the old ways, the old money, and, quite literally, their sacred beliefs. At the heart of this vast conspiracy is the scheming archetypal trickster—whether it is President Obama, the idea of Social Justice, or smarty pants scientists who teach evolution—who manipulate truth as a ruse to gaining true power. Once the trickster succeeds, the world as we know it is imperiled. This trickster must be revealed, deposed, and order restored. But of course under the terms and conditions of this paranoid master narrative, order *can never be* fully restored. For the paranoid there's always another trickster out there waiting to be born, because that is just the way things are.

It's too bad that liberals don't have a core narrative that is so clearly articulated, or a central message that is so clearly defined. Our narrative of progress, by contrast, sounds wimpy. Our narrative—the one Sarah Palin characterizes as "that hopey-changey thing"—is one that equates progress with scientific and humanistic scholarship. From that scholarship, since the Enlightenment, our narrative has inspired women and men to find better ways of solving problems; answering questions; organizing societies; promoting freedom, equality, and justice; and achieving a more complete and compassionate understanding of others. So yeah, Ms. Palin, that "hopey-changey thing" *is* workin' for us. As it is for *all of us*.

But I do understand the narrative challenge: Where's the threat in *that*? Where is the ominous and life-threatening Other? Who is the real enemy?

No wonder, according to recent polls, despite the far right's contention that we represent a "vast conspiracy," our narrative is only strong enough to appeal to 24 percent of the adult population who admits, freely, to being liberal. Ours is, I hate to say it, a failed narrative. What we need to work out is a better one, a more muscular one, one that builds on Barack Obama's foundational principles of *stories* driving the progressive ideas and content. He cannot do it alone. We need to help him, or else it is likely that the extremists' appeal—at home and abroad—will coalesce into a nightmarish vision for America, and one in which we might well find ourselves living in a less than promised land.

So, what to do?

◘

In addition to the advice given earlier about teaching propaganda theory and strategies for combating it, there are clear lessons to be learned from the narrative tactics of the American left in the 1960s. The enemy of the left then, as now, was the Capitalist Corporations (and Banks) that shamelessly overturn lives, communities, and governments for profit. From this narrative perspective, the storyline from the 1960s is that the United States went into Vietnam to rescue Reynolds Aluminum, Goodyear Rubber and other corporations who bought up the French corporate holdings. This narrative had the ring of a conspiracy narrative to it, but for good reason: it was true. History now records the financial facts and damns the collusion of those corporations and many politicians. Then, unfortunately, the narrative thread about the money, about the greed of corporations and banks, about the collusion of politicians, got tangled up with a host of other issues and lost in the streets.

We face the same narrative challenges today. But we can, this time, learn to avoid the narrative errors of the past. What liberals require today is a core narrative that doesn't get sidetracked or diluted or diverted by special interests of small groups and communities. I know that striking an exclusionary tone sounds like an anti-liberal thing to do. But it's true. Before the needs of our special interests can be successfully addressed, we must sell the country on our core narrative. That does not mean giving up the good work done on behalf of social justice, or immigration reform, or gay rights. But it does mean putting the BIG PICTURE narrative first in our hearts and minds. And aligning our actions accordingly.

We must begin with a clear recitation of first principles: *A progressive government can do good things for citizens.* It can be organized to operate efficiently and to protect us from the greed of corporations and banks, and from the anger of extremists near and far. It can promote our health and welfare. It can reinvigorate our schools. But to do those good things our leaders cannot get sidetracked by slanderous attacks on whether our president was born here, or whether Jesus was a socialist, or whether Thomas Jefferson should remain in textbooks.

That is *our* job. Yours and mine. We must go public to combat the threats posed by the ruse of tricksters, these extremist politicians, preachers, and pundits, because they operate in our communities. And because unless we help our president and his administration put out these rhetorical fires, what begins as a dumb-ass propaganda stunt will end up being believed and repeated by enough people to distract all of us from the important progressive work that lies ahead.

The second resource for renewed public engagement with the ideology of near extremism comes from a specialist in combating extremism afar. Heather S. Gregg, of the Naval Postgraduate School, in an article called "Fighting the Jihad of the Pen: Countering Revolutionary Islam's Ideology," posits the following two strategies that we should adopt in our struggle against the ideological narratives on our extreme right. She advocates "helping to magnify the divisions and inconsistencies within revolutionary Islam and helping to create the space and culture of debating ideas."[38]

So, for example, it would seem to follow from Gregg's advice that what liberals should be doing is pointing out the divisions and inconsistencies within extremist rhetoric on the far right, as well as opening up a "marketplace of ideas" to force accountability from their spokespersons and political figures. For example, take the time to find differences that matter between what the Teabaggers say and do; between what the Teabaggers and the conservative Republicans believe and advocate; between local militia groups' websites and how they actually live their lives. Drive wedges into the public spaces where gaps exist or where ideas clash. When Sarah Palin makes bold claims that cannot be supported, don't be content to let pundits be the only ones who take the time to comment on them. Write a letter to the editor. Talk it up. Or post a blog. Circulate the nonsense on Facebook. Use the power of the pen to engage the near jihad.

Throughout this book I have provided resources for accomplishing those ends. I have tried to model what I advocate. Question their presumed authority. Research their statements, track down facts, and make public their propaganda. Again, it may be the case that some of this important work is already done by people like Rachel Maddow or Frank Rich or Arianna Huffington or Bob Herbert. But my call is for *us*—the untelevised, unsyndicated academics—to rise to the public challenge. This work is as important at home as it is abroad because just as it is certainly true that while you will *never* change the extremists' minds, you can and hopefully will influence those who may otherwise be recruited to their cause.

For those who may be new to the idea of "going public," I recommend the three-volume *Communication Activism* anthology edited by Lawrence Frey and Kevin Carragee.[39] If you cannot devote time to complete all three volumes, please read the excellent introduction to volume 1. I also recommend Stephen J. Hartnett's timely and relevant account of what to expect when "going public" means challenging power and those who wield it. Here are a few examples:[40]

- You will receive vicious hate mail, most of it comic, some of it frightening, but all of it discouraging. Responding to this hate mail will initially prove edifying, until you realize that you don't have the slightest chance of changing the minds of most of the bigots who are filling your email in-box. When you come to this realization, it will break your heart.

- You will receive intimidating letters from multinational corporations that believe that threatening you with lawsuits will scare you into silence. The local ACLU and other good lawyers will offer to defend you, but you will still lie in bed at night wondering if strange men-in-suits are coming to get you.

- You will find your scholarly work and political events dissected on blogs, usually by people who have not actually read your work or attended the political events in question. This will of course be devastating, for it will demonstrate that the public sphere has little to do with reason and much to do with ranting-and-raving by fools.

- If you should make the mistake of discussing such matters at faculty brown-bag lunches or cocktail parties, some of your colleagues or acquaintances will look at you in strange ways, suggesting with their awkward glances that you have crossed an unspoken line by raising political questions in what are supposed to be occasions reserved for polite, institutional chatter.

Hartnett goes on to describe other surprises to your routine academic sensemaking system: newspaper editors who cut down your prose and cut out the history sections entirely; news anchors who request that you speak in soundbites; the constant demand to work *quickly*, to blog on the issue *today*, to post that white paper *now*!

I have certainly experienced every one of the insults to integrity and intelligence Hartnett describes, as well as found ways to work for productive change in places that we scholars in the communication field often fear to go: the Department of Defense, the Department of State, various intelligence gathering and analysis agencies; NATO; and other organizations of that ilk. Going public was really the only option for us to gain entry into that world.

The cause of social justice, the cause of peace, the cause of making this blue planet a better, safer, more sustainable place is part of our work in this life. It is a lesson that Scrooge, a learned man, had to learn from the ghost of Jacob Marley, and had to have repeated to him by three more ghosts before he finally got it. Before he *owned* it. Before it haunted him to a new political and social consciousness.

Don't let the Birthers, the anti-Social Justice Beckites, or the Texas Textbook Killers turn you away from your rightfully earned place in the public sphere. You, my fellow academics, have the education, the erudition, and the cleverness to speak out against the tricksters and their toadies. Join with me in promoting the progressive core narrative and take personal responsibility for countering that "hopey-changey thing" slur with stories of actual results.

Remember: it is the story that drives the information. The narrative form the story draws upon and the trajectory it projects for listeners/readers create the appeal. And it is the narrative form of the story plus information widely disseminated that drive progressive change.

4. Left at the War

The Battle of Narratives on Two Fronts: the Global War on Terror and the Right-Wing War on Obama's America

One of the charges made against liberals by conservatives and extremists on the right is that we are soft on war. And one of the great disappointments on the left about the new "liberal" Obama administration is the continuation, and expansion, of the global war on terror in Iraq, Afghanistan, Pakistan, and Yemen. Perhaps even Iran is on the horizon. Who knows? For a man who as senator was brave enough to speak out against the invasion of Iraq, and who campaigned for the presidency on a "bring the troops home by the end of 2009" platform, his actions since taking the oath of office have seemed surprisingly at odds with our hopes.

Viewed differently, however, maybe it is our hopes that are faulty. As Michael Berube puts it in his insider critique of the left, "*We oppose tyranny around the globe, but not to the extent of actually doing anything about it.*"[1] And Berube is not alone. Although everyone on the left rallies against the outright lies and stupidity that defined the Bush administration's invasion of Iraq and subsequent mishandling of every conceivable detail of stabilizing the country and despite the lack of an exit strategy, we are divided about what should be done about it. We are also divided about what should *not* be done about it.

While there is some agreement that the anti-war movement was seized by the Chomsky-ite far left faction in 2002, there is far less agreement about whether the right answer to the question is "stay or come home." No one wants us to stay. But neither do many of us believe that pulling out of the Middle East entirely is the best solution, either. While in theory it makes sense to allow Iraq and Afghanistan to solve their own problems and to redirect the nearly one trillion dollars we have thus far spent over there to addressing a myriad of domestic needs at home, in practice that theoretically pure decision would mean a morally bankrupt outcome. Not only would it enable those who are sworn against us to claim victory, but it would leave in place barely stabilized (Iraq) and corrupt (Afghanistan) governments in charge of an impoverished and illiterate population of over sixty-five million people. That's not saying anything at all about Pakistan, with its nuclear capability, or Yemen, or, God help them, Somalia. So what should we do? What, in fact, *can* be done?

Has the time come for a new liberal voice to rise up and enter the battle of narratives that currently separates not only the right from the left on the war, but also the left from the far left? Could it be the case that Obama's Nobel Prize narrative about the duality of war and peace serves that end? Let's examine, in some detail, how a rational process liberal like Obama sells a war strategy that admits to mistakes, even to our own capacity for evil, but at the same time recognizes our unique role in preventing worst case scenarios from becoming worst case realities.

This is not the narrative Obama or the left has always embraced, but it is a fair assessment of one that has consistently defined the binary opposition drawn between hawks and doves, at least since Vietnam. As Ronald Radosh's excellent review of Peter Beinart's *The Good Fight* puts it:

> The liberal left in America has abandoned its own best heritage for what Arthur Schlesinger Jr. once called "doughface liberal-ism." These liberals oppose terror and totalitarianism but recoil against taking any necessary steps to defeat it, fearful that their moral purity might be stained in the process. . . . He [Beinart] asks nothing less than that liberals (and Democrats) harken back to the much besmirched Cold War liberalism of President Truman, George Kennan, Hubert Humphrey, and others—and move away from the anti-interventionism of Michael Moore, George McGovern, and Howard Dean. The philosophical hero of "The

Good Fight" is Reinhold Niebuhr, a man who gave up on pacifism. Niebuhr posited that Americans have to recognize their own capacity for inflicting evil by building restraints on unmitigated power, but not hesitate to act to prevent greater evils.[2]

Perhaps President Obama is listening to his inner hawk, or perhaps the Department of Defense and its one trillion dollar budget combined with the extremely successful military-industrial complex lobby buys the war voice a larger share of influence. But I prefer to think that while both of those facts are no doubt true, Obama ultimately is following his well-educated liberal conscience. His has been a remarkably consistent voice not necessarily against the war, but certainly on having a clear mission, plan for action, and exit strategy.

In his speech against going to war back in 2002, prior to announcing a bid for the Senate, he said plainly, "I don't oppose all wars. What I am opposed to is a dumb war. What I am opposed to is a rash war."[3] Since that speech and throughout his time in the U.S. Senate and his successful run for the Presidency, Obama has tempered his robust criticism of the conduct of the war, its cost in lives and dollars, and its negative impact on our standing in the world, with a consistent stand in support of the military's role in securing neighborhoods, protecting our embassies, providing humanitarian aid and economic development support, and training local forces. These are not the views of someone who has exchanged peacenik views for those of a hawk since attaining the presidency.

Let's pay some detailed attention to what he said.

Full disclosure: I have been observing and writing about the role of narrative in the Obama war on terror since he took office, beginning with his Cairo address,[4] and culminating (so far) in his Nobel address.[5] Along the way I provided heavy rhetorical and pragmatic criticism of his failed narrative to justify the war when he spoke to the cadets at West Point.[6] But, in my humble opinion, he redeemed himself with the Nobel speech,[7] by opening up an intelligent, muscular narrative framework that Arthur Schlesinger, Jr., would recognize and applaud:

I am the Commander-in-Chief of a nation in the midst of two wars. ... I am responsible for the deployment of thousands of young Americans to battle in a distant land. Some will kill. Some will be killed. And so I come here with an acute sense of the cost of armed conflict—filled with difficult questions about the relationship between war and peace, and our effort to replace one with the other.

In the flawed West Point address that preceded this Nobel oration, President Obama did not cite a moral or political imperative strong enough to support committing more troops, and more lives, to the effort. This time he did, professing a philosophical allegiance to the non-violent leadership of Gandhi and Martin Luther King, Jr., while locating our military commitments to Afghanistan and Iraq within clear instances of intractable historical conflicts that could not have been resolved by peaceful protest or continued negotiations. He said:

A non-violent movement could not have halted Hitler's armies. Negotiations cannot convince al Qaeda's leaders to lay down their arms. To say that force is sometimes necessary is not a call to cynicism—it is a recognition of history; the imperfections of man and the limits of reason.[8]

Effective persuasive speeches rely on a speaker's ability to narrow possible alternative actions needed to solve a problem down to one action favored by the speaker. Usually this is done with a combination of reason and emotion that reveals the character of the speaker to be one who is, as Cicero expressed it, "the good man speaking well." For Obama, this rhetorical end is well accomplished by situating his plan for military action within the universal human struggle against tyranny, genocide, and oppression that could not be resolved in any other way, and then by outlining three goals that all nations must join together to accomplish in order to achieve global security:

1. *A call for unity in opposition to threats against global security*: "Intransigence must be met with increased pressure—and such pressure exists only when the world stands together as one." His example of "increased pressure" includes a continuing commitment to nuclear disarmament, continued pressure

on rogue states, and the application of that same call for united action to places such as Dafur.

2. *A continuing commitment to freedom and human rights*: "So even as we respect the unique culture and traditions of different countries, America will always be a voice for those aspirations that are universal." Obama points out that support for human rights is not the imposition of Western values on other nations, but the realistic application of methods for peace that work—the freedom to speak, to worship, to choose their own leaders, etc. He uses Europe as the example of a region that only came to peace after instituting freedom.

3. *A continued commitment to economic development*: "a just peace includes not only civil and political rights—it must encompass economic security and opportunity. For true peace is not just freedom from fear, but freedom from want."

Beyond cultivating the Ciceronian ideal of "the good man speaking well" with an audience of dedicated peacemakers, the speech reveals what Kenneth Burke calls "identification" between the speaker's values and attitudes and those held by the audience. In addition to the general theme of finding ways to replace war with peace, Obama uses this need for identification by seizing the opportunity to find common ground among all the world's faith traditions:

> We see it in the way that religion is used to justify the murder of innocents by those who have distorted and defiled the great religion of Islam, and who attacked my country from Afghanistan. These extremists are not the first to kill in the name of God; the cruelties of the Crusades are amply recorded. But they remind us that no Holy War can ever be a just war. For if you truly believe that you are carrying out divine will, then there is no need for restraint—no need to spare the pregnant mother, or the medic, or even a person of one's own faith. Such a warped view of religion is not just incompatible with the concept of peace, but the purpose of faith—for the one rule that lies at the heart of every major religion is that we do unto others as we would have them do unto us.

This speech opens *narrative* possibilities by opening up themes that most leaders leave out of speeches: e.g., the relationship of war to religion. You may recall that President Bush went to great pains to separate the "war on terror" from "a war on Muslims," but further bifurcation only produced the strong belief among the world's Muslims that this lack of distinction might, in fact, be the case. Splitting definitional hairs over binary oppositions only works if the speaker has credibility. Bush had almost none at the time, and so his attempt to separate the ideas of war and religion only served to unite them.

By contrast, throughout the Nobel address Obama, who does have credibility, juxtaposes binary oppositions built from the war/peace trope, showing those terms, in fact, to be not binary oppositions at all but *part of a larger and more complex dualism that defines the human condition*, and for which we are still seeking solutions: "The instruments of war do have a role to play in preserving the peace.... So part of our challenge is reconciling these two seemingly irreconcilable truths—that war is sometimes necessary, and war is at some level an expression of human feelings." In other words, war and peace are not necessarily in opposition to one another. They are as inextricably bound together in human history as our emotions are bound to our ability to reason.

Furthermore, Obama challenges the idea that peace may be accomplished without sacrifice: "I also know this: the belief that peace is desirable is rarely enough to achieve it. Peace requires responsibility. Peace entails sacrifice." Having already admitted that his moral compass was heavily influenced by the non-violent work of Gandhi and King, Jr., he complicates the rhetorical divide of peace/violence with this observation: "We do not have to think that human nature is perfect for us to still believe that the human condition can be perfected. We do not have to live in an idealized world to still reach for those ideals that will make it a better place."

This message is the core principle of a decidedly liberal narrative of history: that we were born in a violent struggle and through sacrifice we move forward, we make progress toward our best ideals—freedom, justice for all, peace, equality under the law, economic and intellectual opportunity. By contrast, the core principle of a conservative narrative of history goes something like this: we were born great and have only to return to those first principles of the Founding Fathers to retain our greatness. Between these two competing visions lies the battleground of the American narrative.

One side believes in a *literal interpretation* of the Constitution and a literal interpretation of the *Holy Bible*. The other side believes that *consequences* of both adherence to first principles—whatever their source—and interpreting them within the changed historical, economic, and social conditions of today warrant debate. Obama is clearly an interpretivist, and as such his warrant is always one forged between where we are and where we want to be, between a reality of the here and now and "the audacity of hope" for a better future and against a very real future composed of worst case scenarios.

At the end of the speech he returns to the theme of war and peace—never far removed from the substance of the talk—and says this:

> We can acknowledge that oppression will always be with us, and still strive for justice. We can admit the intractability of deprava-tion, and still strive for dignity. We can understand that there will be war, and still strive for peace. We can do that—for that is the story of human progress; that is the hope of all the world; and at this moment of challenge, that must be our work here on Earth.

Notice that he turns all binary oppositions into mutually depen-dent dualisms or tensions, a ying and yang of the human condition. In so doing, President Obama offers us a way to think about a way to move the narrative that was defined by binary oppositions (us versus them, Crusaders versus Islam, etc.) to a new *ternary framing*. Perhaps in his stark and compelling narrative on war given to an audience for peace, he found the perfect context to complicate our thinking about our role in the global war on terror and the responsibilities as well as the opportunities that liberals bring to the challenge.

In particular, the role liberal educators—and, according to the far right, there is no other kind—should willingly play in "actually doing something about it," say, by bringing the academic theories and research tools we own to bear in order to forge a new understand-ing—a muscular liberal understanding—of the central and defining role of narratives in this global war of ideas.

Military leaders and presidents seldom admit that a war cannot be won. So imagine the world's surprise when, on September 28, 2009, General Stanley McChrystal told CNN: "If the people are against us, we cannot be successful. If the people view us as occupiers and the enemy, we can't be successful and our casualties will go up dramatically."[9]

This statement echoes similar sentiments expressed by Secretary Robert Gates, Joint Chiefs Chairman Mike Mullen, and General David Patraeus about the global war on terror not being simply about kinetics, but about ideas; not solely about weapons of mass destruction, but about weapons of mass persuasion. This enlightened view of what it takes to win a war of ideas, to be triumphant in the battle of narratives, is most succinctly summed up in President Obama's speech in Phoenix in August 2009: "Because in the twenty-first century, military strength will be measured not only by the weapons our troops carry, but by the languages they speak and the cultures they understand."[10]

Collectively our military leaders recognize that "winning the hearts and minds" of a local population is key to strategic success, especially when a large part of that success depends on safe and secure neighborhoods, functioning institutions, and an infrastructure capable of supporting a fledgling democracy. That's a liberal vision of progress that recognizes, fully, the limits of traditional military power as well as our need to work against those worse case scenarios coming true.

So, given this need, what is the work that must be done? How is it best to "win the hearts and minds" of Others who might otherwise be persuaded to not only rail against our policies and the negative influence of the West, but also to use all available means of persuasion—including violence—to leverage their message, their narrative, against us?

Paul Berman, author of the well-regarded *Terror and Liberalism* (2003) and perhaps the leading "liberal hawk" in America today, believes that the promotion of democracy—while done badly in every respect by the Bush administration—is still a good idea in the Middle East because without it, we end up promoting dictatorships or standing by idly watching law and order decay.

Berman also points out that no sense of democracy is likely to work unless both liberals and conservatives do some important "intellectual work," specifically, until we learn to *understand the people and cultures* that make up the region:

> In the West, an amazing number of people remain biased in one fashion or another against Muslims and especially against Arabs—remain attached to the notion that Arabs cannot reach a level of civilization that is capable of producing democracy. There is a right-wing way of expressing this particular bias, but also a left-wing way, having to do with multiculturalism, which leads people to conclude that if the Arab world is awash in paranoid doctrines and grotesque dictatorships, we mustn't judge anyone harshly, and who are we to say that liberalism and prosperity are superior to tyranny and poverty, and aren't some of those paranoias true, and so on? In this manner, left-wing tolerance and right-wing intolerance end up oddly resembling each other. A first component of our effort, then, should be to shed light on the unfair and cruel assumptions that so many people make about the Arab world, and sometimes about other parts of the Muslim world, as well.[11]

It was this sort of reasoning that may have led Secretary Gates to sponsor and fund three new programs designed to promote cultural understanding among the military and diplomatic personnel assigned to the Middle East. Or it may have been his recognition that "kinetic solutions"—relying solely on things that go BANG!—are not going to be successful in our quest to bring stability to failed states and war-ravaged nations in the Middle East. As a general succinctly expressed it to me: "We can't kill all of 'em." As any soldier who has spent time in the region will tell you, for every civilian casualty we inflict—whether from an accident or drone or mistaken intelligence or poor judgment—we directly contribute to the appeal of, and to the spread of, violent extremism. So while our military presence and action may be necessary in the short-term, for long-term peace and stability, if that is possible, it is better to seek non-kinetic solutions.

The first program—and easily the most controversial—has been the Human Terrain System (HTS) under the leadership of retired special forces colonel Steve Fondacaro and cultural anthropologist Dr. Montgomery McFate.[12] This program embedded anthropologists and other social scientists with military units in Iraq and Afghanistan. The teams consisted of two civilians and three military personnel, and the objective was for the civilians to provide the military with information while, at the same time, lessening the tensions with local populations. Although the program of enhanced cultural understanding is acknowledged everywhere as a good idea and is still a cornerstone of the COIN (Counter Insurgency) plan, the HTS project demonstrated the very real problems of placing civilians into war zones. As of this writing, four social scientists have been killed in action, one taken hostage, and two have been wounded.

Beyond death and injury to the scientists, the project has also been criticized for poor methods of data collection in "combat ethnography"—pejoratively labeled "mercenary ethnography" for its uneven record of differentiating between information useful to building cultural knowledge and that which is useful to the military in targeting civilian populations.

The second program designed to enhance cultural understanding useful to the military consists of the Department of Defense five-year interdisciplinary team research grants, known as MINERVA, of upwards of fifty million dollars.[13] The first round of awards consists of the following projects:

Fy 2009 Minerva Research Initiative — Winners of Technical Competition

(PI) Project Title

- Susan Shirk, University of California, San Diego, "The Evolving Relationship Between Technology and National Security in China: Innovation, Defense Transformation, and China's Place in the Global Technology Order"

- Mark Woodward, Arizona State University, "Finding Allies for the War of Words: Mapping the Diffusion and Influence of Counter-Radical Muslim Discourse"

- Patricia Lewis, Monterey Institute of International Studies, "Iraq's Wars with the U.S. from the Iraqi Perspective: State Security, Weapons of Mass Destruction, Civil-Military Relations, Ethnic Conflict and Political Communication in Baathist Iraq"

- Jacob Shapiro, Princeton University, "Terrorism Governance and Development"

- David Matsumoto, San Francisco State University, "Emotion and Intergroup Relations"

- James Lindsay, The University of Texas at Austin, "Climate Change, State Stability, and Political Risk in Africa"

- Nazli Choucri, Massachusetts Institute of Technology, "ECIR— Explorations in Cyber International Relations"

I list these awards to lessen some of the mystery surrounding Department of Defense (DOD) projects developed under the Minerva program. Each one of them—by mandate from the DOD—is a basic research project. There is no intention of the personnel involved in the grants to apply anything. It's about discovering and creating knowledge. It's what academics are supposed to do.

The Office of Naval Research administers the third project. Generally organized under the Broad Area Announcements (BAA) aegis, Area I of the project is dedicated to "Understanding the Human, Social, Cultural, and Behavioral Influences." The Consortium for Strategic Communication at Arizona State University won one of these awards in the Spring of 2009, for a project called "Identifying and Countering Extremist Narratives." Like the HTS and MINERVA projects, the aim of the project is to provide useful information about cultures to the military. Unlike HTS, the researchers are not embedded with military units in Iraq or Afghanistan.

These projects reflect what we as academics are trained to do and should be doing: research and write in our area of expertise, and publish our results. Our expertise is drawn from scholars who specialize in narrative, cultures, and media. Researchers (of which I am one) at CSC are constructing a new—and dare I say it, *innovative*— way to think about narratives in relation to extremist ideology, then build a database of master cultural narratives, current narratives, and narrative fragments in circulation in Indonesia, the Middle East, and North Africa/Southern Europe. From that database we will eventually build an agent-based modeling system that combines the sensitivities of our humanities-based approach to narratives with a more traditional scientific approach to modeling and predicting which narratives in circulation are likely to be troublesome in the region. It's all speculative, theoretical, and cutting-edge stuff that is made possible because it asks big questions that may only be adequately addressed by bringing together an interdisciplinary team representing humanistic and scientific scholars.

Our research will find its way into the top journals in our field, into books published by academic presses, will be disseminated via traditional academic conferences and will appear on our website.[14] It has an additional benefit of providing useful cultural information and advice about communication to our military forces in harm's way. Put differently, we are promoting cultural understanding as one non-kinetic solution to the ongoing challenges in the targeted regions. We are helping to make peace, not war, while recognizing and responding responsibly to the duality of war and peace in our world.

Now to the inevitable question raised by my colleagues and friends on the left: does my participation in such a project compromise my liberal values? Not at all. But it does complicate them.[15] Using what I know about communication, and what our team can find out through academic research into the work of narratives in cultures to help the women and men who serve our country in uniform is a good thing. But it doesn't make my anger about the secrecy, stupidity, and lies of the Bush administration any less acute, nor does it make my personal belief that the current struggle in Afghanistan and Pakistan is likely to be a long slog that we can ill afford any less of a belief. My liberal values, my progressive narrative, my commitment to peace are all still firmly in place.

What it does mean is that because I am paid to read and think about ways to combat terrorism I have become far less uninformed, far less politically naïve, than I used to be about the real threat posed by the global social movement spawned by al Qaeda's dangerous and corrupt, Islam-warping, extremist ideology.

What it does mean is that I have become far more knowledgeable about the Taliban.

And about the Qur'an. And the philosopher of al Qaeda, Sayyid Qtub's, interpretation of it.[16]

I have learned to hear in the speeches of radical clerics and propagandists for extremist groups in the UK, in Germany, in Yemen, as well as in these United States, the echoes of old sacred stories that, viewed one way, offer lessons about hope to true believers, and that when viewed differently twist those same old stories to preach a violent jihad and offer seventy-two virgins for every martyr's sacrifice. Finding ways to counter the latter message while preserving the former one is vital to the health and welfare of the world.

For me, it is akin to using what I know to help find a cure for a deadly virus that spreads principally although not exclusively among the young, targeting their brains and manipulating their bodies, without resorting to injecting something equally dangerous into them. Something, say, kinetic. Something that goes BANG!

Most of my friends on the left understand and support that cause. It is "the good fight," even if it is a bad war. It is also a necessary fight, especially for those of us who do not want to see this nation repeat, out of ignorance and fear, or out of a desire for revenge, the political and military mistakes of the immediate past. They agree that the politics of fear perpetrated by a campaign of propaganda from the Bush administration gave birth to new forms and formats of mediated communication, a frightening blur of popular culture and social control enabled by extremist narratives and explicit visual images.[17]

However, I readily admit that there are also those of the far left who find any help I might be able to provide to the military in the battle against extremism to be simply, and decidedly, *wrong*. To be abhorrent to them. These are often very bright people, very talented individuals. They are, no doubt, the clever clogs who would use the analogy above—that fighting terrorism is like trying to find a cure for a virus that targets the minds and bodies of the young—and say the real enemy is *capitalism*, which does much the same thing. Who would add to that indictment that America has engaged in terrorist acts and that we have violated human rights.

And they would be intellectually and perhaps even morally correct. The duality of capitalism is that it frees and kills, liberates and oppresses. And yes, America is still a work in progress and we are still struggling to live with those better angels of our spirit and the true worth of our values.

But, in my humble opinion, clever lefty criticism is largely beside the point when it comes to taking on the battle against violent extremism. Giving voice to protest may be carried out as an act of resistance and my friends opposed to the war have every right to it. But what does it do to help prevent the spread of violent extremism?[18] What does it do to prevent the wolf at the back door from entering our own homes?

For you see, we *are* the enemy. We are the apostate intellectuals. Perhaps you are gay or lesbian. You are definitely marked for death. Likely you have only a thin connection to your faith tradition, which these days you may practice once in awhile. Claiming to be "sort of" a Person of the Book won't spare you. You will be offered a one-time chance to convert (although technically, Osama bin Laden offered America that deal back in 1998 in his "Letter to America," and again in 2002, and my guess is you didn't take it). If you refuse, you die. It's really that simple. That is the plan.

Still doubt me? Consider the following statement, made in early March 2010 by a nice American boy from Las Cruces, New Mexico, now an al Qaeda spokesperson operating under the moniker Anwar al-Awlaki, who has been preaching violence against America since 2006:[19]

> To the Muslims in America, I have this to say: How can your conscience allow you to live in peaceful co-existence with a nation that is responsible for the tyranny and crimes committed against your own brothers and sisters?
>
> With the American invasion of Iraq and continued U.S. aggression against Muslims, I could not reconcile between living in the U.S. and being a Muslim, and I eventually came to the conclusion that jihad against America is binding upon myself, just as it is binding on every other Muslim.[20]

This is the same American son whose website and email messages have been implicated in Major Nidal Hussan's murder spree at Ft. Hood, and before that, he served as a "spiritual advisor" to two of the 9/11 hijackers, Nawaf al-Hamzi and Hani Hanjour. In March 2010, President Obama authorized his targeted killing, the first American citizen in our history to hold that dubious distinction.

Or how about a nice Jewish boy from Southern California, Adam Gadahn (born Adam Pearlman), who works as a cultural interpreter, spokesperson, and media advisor to al Qaeda?[21] On October 11, 2006, he was charged with treason against the United States following a September video in which he invited Americans to convert to Islam or die.

Fortunately, there are, to date, only a few examples of the jihad mentality evident within the post 9/11 United States of America. But those that have occurred are nevertheless instructive. Major Hussan, Adam Gadahn and Anwar al-Awlaki have already been cited. But do you know the case of Colleen LaRose, aka JihadJane, a petit, blonde, forty-six-year-old Main Street, Pennsburg, Pennsylvania, resident who is linked with seven jihadists in Ireland, who used her U.S. website to raise money for a plot to murder "an unbeliever," a *kufar*, Lars Vilks, who had drawn a political cartoon depicting Mohammad's head atop a dog.[22] Or the singular case of one Joseph Stack, a fifty-three year-old software engineer who, on February 18, 2010, flew his plane into the IRS building in Austin, Texas, killing, in addition to his sad ass, two people?[23]

While the latter two examples do not fit the typical profile of a terrorist, both LaRosa and Stack engaged in terrorist activities designed to kill people for a cause. For one of them, that cause was the radical fundamentalism of Islamism, for the other it was the radical fundamentalism of an anti-tax, anti-government extremism. What they share in common is a commitment to extreme political action on behalf of their beliefs and a core narrative of self-justification. What they lack, both of them, is empathy or respect for the common humanity of those who they would, or did, kill.

One of their victims could have just as easily been you. Had your paths crossed. Had your day, your life, found its final sum in their anger. They would not see you as a human being, a child of God, or even as someone who didn't deserve to die. For violent jihadis, taking human lives is often indiscriminate. Designed to inspire fear and panic. That's the textbook definition of terrorism.

What extremists lack is any openness to argument, to dialogue, to civil discourse, to finding some other peaceful solution to their grievances. For them, an act of violence carries the only message they care to send. Their preferred ends cannot be negotiated or debated. They are absolute.

I know what you are thinking. You are thinking that we have yet to move into an era where violent solutions dominate the political landscape. You are thinking that our time is not even unique in American history. And you would be correct. For example, Dennis Lehane's masterful novel, *Any Given Day*, provides a profound historical parallel between these troubled times and what was happening in America at the end of World War I, including attempted assassinations of the attorney general by an IED (improvised explosive device); anarchists' attacks on buildings and police; police at war with each other over unions; racial and class conflicts so deep that they tore apart families, cities, and the nation.

Nor do we have to turn the pages of history back quite that far to recall, vividly, the political violence and assassinations of the 1960s. While there are historical parallels that remind us that our country has *always* been defined by citizens speaking out against the government, by groups fighting against each other for some political or social end, by lone gunmen and crazies bent on violence, I do think that the mood and tenor of the political debate today, its raw corrosive anger and threatened as well as real violence, while not unique, is certainly worthy of our worry. And our action.

There are wolves at our door. One is a far enemy, and one is a near enemy.

Both of those enemies are busy defining in extremist terms the nature of the future they desire for us. That, if left unchecked, they intend to visit upon us. So no, John Boehner (R-OH), minority leader of the 111th House of Representatives, Armageddon is *not* just a word. I think most Americans understand that, which is why everyone was appalled at your use of it to launch the final, failed attacks on health care reform. Your lame defense—that "Armageddon is just a word"—was disingenuous.

Americans also understand that when Sarah Palin on her Facebook page used target imagery drawn from gun sights to urge supporters to "reload" for the fall elections,[24] she was simply behaving as a dumb-ass. But I can't believe that Ms. Palin, as clueless as she appears to be, honestly believes that assassination of the opposition is the way to win elections. It was just a tasteless metaphor, not a true analogy.

But I do think most Americans do not understand how serious a threat the near enemy poses. The loosely connected network of near extremists. In March 2010 the Southern Poverty Law Center released its annual report on hate:

> Since the installation of Barack Obama, right-wing extremists have murdered six law enforcement officers. Racist skinheads and others have been arrested in alleged plots to assassinate the nation's first black president. One man from Brockton, Mass.— who told police he had learned on white supremacist websites that a genocide was under way against whites—is charged with murdering two black people and planning to kill as many Jews as possible on the day after Obama's inauguration. Most recently, a rash of individuals with antigovernment, survivalist or racist views have been arrested in a series of bomb cases.
>
> As the movement has exploded, so has the reach of its ideas, aided and abetted by commentators and politicians in the ostensible mainstream. While in the 1990s, the movement got good reviews from a few lawmakers and talk-radio hosts, some of its central ideas today are being plugged by people with far larger audiences like Fox News's Glenn Beck and U.S. Rep. Michele Bachmann (R-Minn). Beck, for instance, re-popularized a key Patriot conspiracy theory—the charge that FEMA is secretly running concentration camps—before finally "debunking" it.[25]

Or consider what Lee Siegel calls "The New Republican War Room," which is a "right of center" large scale political blog run by Erick Erickson of Georgia under the title Redstate.com and dedicated to starting a conservative revolution: "Ladies and Gentlemen, I submit to you again that it is not enough to just throw out the Democrats in favor of Republicans. We must throw out the Democrats and replace them with the right kind of Republicans—conservatives who actually are conservative."[26]

What makes this blog so interesting is its ordinary exterior, an appearance of rationality in the service of the conservative cause: "There's a calm, understated visual setting that expresses a fiery sentiment: a red map of America overlapping with white stars on a blue field. It projects the sense of rebellious feelings inspired yet also contained by patriotic piety. These are serious Americans out to rescue America from its enemies."[27] Erickson was invited to the White House in 2006 by George Bush. Eric Cantor announced his campaign for Republican minority whip on Restate.com. Erickson himself has appeared on *Morning Joe*.

Yet there is something wrong here. Something amiss. Something that doesn't quite add up. It is as if an actor with a soothing voice is simply explaining why it is necessary to eliminate us. He's smiling, he's bright enough, but ultimately, his message is scary.

But not nearly as scary as some other voices out there in the blogosphere. Consider militia leader Mike Vanderboegh of Pinson, Alabama, leader of a group called the Three Percenters. John Avlon, political columnist and author of *Wingnuts: How the Lunatic Fringe is Hijacking America*, describes the militia and their goals this way:

> The Three Percenters, [is] one of the threefold increase in militia groups—I call them "Hatriot" groups—that has sprung up in the first 15 months of the Obama administration, as detailed by the Southern Poverty Law Center. They take their name from the questionable statistic that only three percent of the American colonists actively fought for independence. Therefore, the Three Percenters position themselves both as an elite group and also a direct link to the Founding Fathers, making their extremist alienation from mainstream America a badge of honor and secret knowledge. They describe themselves as "promoting the ideals of liberty, freedom and a constitutional government restrained by law."
>
> Vanderbeough has warned his supporters to prepare for what he calls "The Big Die Off": "When a computer crashes, you simply discard it and obtain another. When political systems, nations or civilizations fail, they collapse in a welter of blood and

carnage, usually ending in mountains of bodies, slavery and a long dark night of tyranny. This is referred to by people today who recognize the existential danger by the short-hand acronym of 'TBDO'—'The Big Die Off.' This is not a video game. There are no do-overs. This is as real as it gets. Your system has experienced one or more fatal errors and must shut down at this time. Whether you survive The Big Die Off with anything left that is worth preserving is up to you."[28]

Avlon reports that Vanderbeough was responsible for posting a blog advocating violence against those who voted for health care reform. On his "Sipsey Street Irregulars" blog Vanderbeough wrote: "If we break the windows of hundreds, thousands, of Democrat party headquarters across this country, we might just wake up enough of them to make defending ourselves at the muzzle of a rifle unnecessary." As Avlon correctly observes, "the parallels, intentional or not, to the Nazis' heinous 1938 kristallnacht, or 'Night of Broken Glass,' so-named for the 7,000 storefront windows that were smashed, are hard to ignore."[29]

Then there is The Doctrine of the Three Percent:

The Three Percent are the folks the Founders counted on
to save the Republic when everyone else abandoned it.

And we will.

There will be no more free Wacos and no more free Katrinas.

For we are the Three Percent.

We will not disarm.

You cannot convince us.

You cannot intimidate us.

You can try to kill us, if you think you can.

But remember, we'll shoot back.

We are not going away.

We are not backing up another inch.

And there are THREE MILLION OF US.

Your move, Mr. Wannabe Tyrant.

Your move.[30]

All of that precedes Vanderbeough's final comment, a quotation from one Billy Beck in August of 2009: "All politics in this country now is just dress rehearsal for civil war."

Then there is the singular case of Reverend Fred Phelps of the Topeka, Kansas, based Westboro Baptist Church. This church has been identified as a "hate group" by the Southern Poverty Law Center for its open and unparalleled attacks on gays and vocal protests at the funerals of AIDS victims and soldiers.[31] According to the *Roanoke Times*, "The group views the deaths of soldiers overseas and other tragedies as proof of God's disdain for America. Followers have said that President Obama is the biblical Antichrist and called on Jews to repent for the killing of Jesus."[32]

This is not a church. It is a terrorist cell. It is a malignancy on the body and spirit of freedom.

The extremist rhetoric calling for a violent revolution against groups they oppose on political and religious grounds reminds me of the radical calls to insurgency following the breakdown of the government and infrastructure in Iraq after the U.S.-led invasion. Over there, of course, the insurgents have historical tribal identifications. Over here those "tribal identities" are digitally manufactured and electronically networked, created out of blogs like Erickson's, or Vanderbeough's, or Facebook pages like Palin's, or websites such as that of the Westboro Baptist Church.[31]

One more word about Sarah Palin's "targeting" of candidates in the fall 2010 elections. And let's assume—because I do—that she was simply displaying dumb-ass taste in choosing that term. The fact is that the lady in black leather is *influential*. As political columnist Mona Gable put it:

This week we've seen that words like these have terrifying consequences. In an interview with *The National Review* John Boehner suggested that Steve Driehaus, a freshman Democrat from Cincinnati, would be a "dead man" if he voted for health care. Driehaus did, and now his family has received death threats. New York Democrat Louise Slaughter received a message saying snipers were going to kill the children of all those who'd voted for health care. Imagine walking outside your house one morning to find a coffin there. That happened to Missouri Democrat Ross Carnahan.

Republican leaders have yet to firmly denounce these threats. I guess they're afraid of looking wimpy or weak and want to keep their jobs. It's no wonder Palin feels emboldened to demean Obama and attack Democrats with no regard for the consequences. It's clear she doesn't care, that she's willing to say anything. Let's not forget: this is the college graduate who couldn't even tell Katie Couric what newspapers she reads. So it's not like she has a regard for language or facts.

With thousands of angry followers on Facebook and Twitter, Palin might no longer hold office, but she's still holding court. And that combined with her almost gleeful ignorance makes her dangerous. It's time to call Palin out and hold her accountable.[34]

So there we have it. It *is* time to hold Palin et al. accountable. It is time to speak out against the Three Percenters, the Teabaggers, the Keep America Safers, Fred Phelps, the oath-keepers, and the rest of the far right extremists. They all belong to essentially the same "armed and dangerous" tribe of gun-toting rabble-rousers, and they do mean us harm. There can be no doubt of that.

We must take them at their word, even if some of them claim they weren't being literal:[35] Reload. Targeted. Armageddon. Dead man.

We must remember that members of their ilk have already murdered law officers, attempted assassinations, broken windows, planted bombs, disrupted soldiers' and AIDS victims' funerals, called the president the Antichrist, spit on elected officials, used vicious racial and ethnic slurs, delivered death threats, claimed God was on their side, and said that if they are challenged, they promise "to shoot back." They believe that the freedoms and beliefs of the majority in our democracy are disposable and only apply to a few, to them, to the less than 12 percent of the population that thinks like them. They propose in their pamphlets, on their blogs, and through their talking points to deny the other roughly 85-90 percent of the population who vote and work and go to school our democratic freedoms either by electing Tea Party members, or, if necessary, by force.

Connect the dots. How much more warning do the rest of us need? There are days when I wonder if we learned anything from the far enemy's extremist's rhetorical and kinetic lead-up to 9/11. Now we see the same escalating pattern of righteous hate and obscene demands from the near enemy. Are we simply awaiting a spectacular event to make their plans any clearer? Is that what it would take?

I fear it is.

What the far right is counting on is our complacency. Our desire to be well-liked by everyone, our need to be or at least appear to be bipartisan and fair. Our belief in the freedom of speech and respect for the opinions of others in our always-contentious, multivocal democracy. It is precisely these liberal values, and holding on to them despite a public electoral mandate to get things done, that has allowed a dysfunctional Congress turn into a failed one. All in the name of bipartisanship, in the name of fairness, when in reality what we should have learned by now is that *the far right has no interest in bipartisanship.* They see negotiation and compromise as a sign of weakness. The only thing they understand is power. So when the Democrats finally figured out that despite the lies, stalls, false hope, and innuendo, none of the Republicans were going to vote for the health care reform bill, they got busy and passed it anyway. Imagine that! We could defeat the extremists! It was our party now.

And it felt good. Very good indeed. But health care reform was only one battle, one that was not without its casualties. But this battle is, as Donald Rumsfeld characterized the Global War on Terror, "an enduring war." That means there is no end in sight. It also means that everything has changed as a result of it. Over there in the Middle East, we continue to wage war, against the far enemy, in a war against non-state actors. But over here, at home, we wage war against the near enemy, against one another. It resembles the rhetorical build up to our own Civil War. And these right wing hate groups should remind us those bands of popular sloganeers, paid propagandists, political shills, armed night raiders, and bloody insurrectionists that fueled the flames of violent nineteenth century revolution.

It is a familiar, if deceptive, scenario. Yes, some of the same themes are in play. And yes, there are far more cultural differences than similarities between then and now, as if we were comparing bullet trains to buggies, where the point of comparison is not just about the speed of the technology or the reach of the imagination, but instead about our entire perception of reality as defined by the ultimate end game—moving forward or falling back. The end game never changes.

What was real then is much the same now as it was then: narratives held together less by empirical facts than by a shared sense of political purpose. And what is important is being decided less by freedom than by our worst fears.

All revolutions are battles of narratives, moved into action not by centers that hold us together but by extremes that tear us apart.

The one tribe in this battle, the one domestic tribe that seems not to have recognized the dual nature of the extremist problem and their own naïve complicity in it—and it pains me to say so—is the American far left.

People on the far left of the political spectrum are as much to blame for narrative extremism as the rhetorical radicals on the far right. What these otherwise well-intentioned citizens on the far left ought to recognize is that their smarty pants French criticism and "just say no" approach to Obama's continuation of the war effort at home and abroad not only echoes what Osama bin Laden wants, but also serves the longer-term political interests of the far right. By compromising the moral legitimacy of a new muscular left—and the narrative of progress it rightfully serves—the far left encourages the vast majority of Americans in the center and on the right to retreat to their comfortable oppositional soundbites: that we liberals (and Democrats) are soft on terrorism; that the left hates the military; that we are all Socialists or Commies (or to Glenn Beck's mind, Nazis *and* Commies *and* Socialists). And so on.

Clinging to the old far left habit of disorganized but loud and often disruptive opposition doesn't change minds.

The citizens in the center are made afraid by them. Other liberals are made ashamed by them. Only the right benefits from far left rhetoric. But here's the problem: the far right narrative is not too far removed from the mainstream right's espoused values—flag-waving patriotism, small federal government, states rights, no taxes, rugged individualism, love my guns, love my Jesus, and (as far as I can tell) a confused foreign policy that is one part dogged isolationism and two parts military power.

By contrast, the relationship of the far left to the mainstream left and center is highly problematic. Those on the far left, like their ideological opposites on the far right, stand against anything but total acceptance of their extreme political position. On health care, polls showed that the far left was opposed to any compromise, including the ones in the final bill. On the war, they—following Noam Chomsky's lead—prefer to revel in what's wrong with America rather than what can be done to oppose the extremism and totalitarianism represented by the Taliban (whether Islamist or Christian) or al Qaeda.

In public the far left is either ridiculed or ignored. Mainstream liberals are tarred with the same broad brush, which is one reason why only a fifth of the American adult population claims an affiliation with us. And even those low numbers of professed liberals would be okay if the feckless far left didn't tar the rest of us with the widespread if false suspicion that all those of us anywhere on the left can do is to promote "anti-American" values and beliefs.

Basically, it's the same narrative challenge that we face in combating al Qaeda and the Taliban: an over-reliance on binary oppositions and narrative IEDs. Us versus Them. Crusaders versus Infidels. Good versus Evil. This point doesn't negate the necessity of using those tools when they fit. For example, I use the terms "enemies" and "dumb-asses" routinely to describe those near and far extremists who do, in fact, threaten to destroy the American progress narrative as well as the American way of life. But I do not use those terms lightly, nor do I apply them broadly.

Our narrative revolution requires a clear separation of progressive liberals from the extremist Crusaders on the far left. Otherwise, finding ways to recapture the beautiful idea of America from the dumb-asses on the far right will not succeed. To attain this separation won't be easy. It is analogous to the rhetorical challenge of separating "moderate" Muslims ("progressive" is a much better label) from extremists, and jihadists from, as Jarrett Brachman in his book *Global Jihadism: Theory and Practice* (2008) names them, "jihobbyists."[36]

Which is to say we have to introduce subtlety, nuance, and a new politics of difference into the battle of narratives, as well as make occasional use of ridicule and humor. Sometimes, as in the case of the "jihobbyist" label, combine the two. Only then will we make progress. Narrative progress.

There is a third player in this Battle of Narratives. I think of it as akin to "Shaytan," the Islamic version of Satan, who in their faith tradition is more of a trickster than a god. Shaytan accomplishes evil by whispering into ears, by encouraging bad practices such as drinking wine and gambling. Devout Muslims pray five times a day and part of their daily prayer is to ask Allah to protect them from Shaytan's whispers. The rest of us should learn from their example.

In America, Shaytan works through ring wing "entertainment news." When Rupert Murdoch infected the United States with this ring wing brand of "news," the radical right here (as in England and on the Continent) was very quick to see the opening it provided by stretching free speech beyond any earlier limits. Furthermore, viewership on Fox and readership of the *Wall Street Journal* increased dramatically because the sensationalism masquerading as "breaking news" was whispered into our ears with a continuous streaming narrative that posits an extremist worldview: a world in chaos and disorder, one defined by political division, corruption, lies, and giving us all good reason for suspicion of true motives at the highest levels of government, aided and abetted by a clear and present lack of True Faith, and by a clear and present lack of respect for Our Constitution, coming from an Aussie owner who has no vested interested in America other than the financial gains to be made from rising ratings and the ad revenue ratings bring in.

We are, as a nation of over-mediated news gawkers, lazy fact-checkers, and sexual dupes, seduced by singularly attractive salacious females dressed in designer clothes who lure those on the right with their siren song of fairness and balance. These screen gems are mostly faux-blonde white girls with good legs and fine cleavage who willingly and knowingly say the most incredible and generally not entirely true things with absolute confidence and obvious allure. As the postmodern among us recognize, we live life at velocity speed and as a result trust only in surfaces. Men and women alike want to believe in surfaces, no matter what those surfaces say! Why? Because, as Elaine Walster, G. William Walster, and Ellen Bersheid demonstrated to the social science community through a series of excellent experiments in the 1970s, in America "we often confuse the beautiful with the true."[37]

It was—it is—Shaytan's handiwork. Appeal to our emotions, our fears, our patriotism, our hypersexuality, and our money, our love, and our votes will follow.

For Murdoch/Beck/Palin/Limbaugh and others of their ilk, the object and purpose of their narrative is to extend their own personal wealth, and by their fanning the flames of extremist tensions, and it works: more money rolls in everyday. These mediated Shaytans can afford to flee if civil strife begins, while no doubt continuing to collect capital made on the sorrow of the nation. This third social force in the Battle of Narratives must be acknowledged for what it is: *The Great Enabler of Extremism*. Media are the primary disseminators of political narratives, and when they are controlled by Capitalists-gone-amuck, we must find some counterforce short of censorship.

One way we can do that is to introduce legislation barring the ownership of U.S. media firms by foreigners. Get Murdoch out. If this idea seems outlandish to you, think back to a few years ago when a Chinese firm came close to buying one of our major ports. What did Congress do? Recognizing the threat of foreign control over an important American asset—to say nothing of the national security issues involved—they passed a bill forbidding it. It seems to me that foreign ownership of our media poses a far greater national security threat than one of our ports.

Oh, you quip, that wouldn't work! Murdoch would just find someone with an American birth certificate to be his puppet. Perhaps so. But that puppet would be personally subject to American laws and regulations. More importantly, we should reconsider the wisdom of the 1996 Telecommunications Act, the seemingly innocent goal of which was "to let anyone enter any communications business—to let any communications business compete in any market against any other,"[38] and investigate ways to expand the authority accorded to the Public Safety and Homeland Security mission of the Federal Communications

Commission to ensure more than just our ability to restore the media infrastructure after a terrorist attack or natural disaster.

I call this chapter "Left at the War" for two reasons. First, because the global war on terror is a battleground of competing narratives that brings to bear political and ideological differences on what I consider a profound and enduring challenge to the stability and security of the world. What the Bush administration left us—left us at the war and on the narrative battlefield—was a legacy of focused wrongness, and, because of the illegal actions they sponsored or endorsed, we are at a serious disadvantage in the battle to win hearts and minds. Put simply, under the Bush administration world opinion of the United States was at its lowest point *ever*.[39] Most of the world—including our allies—thought our message lacked credibility and that our actions did not accord with our professed values. Since President Obama took office, there has been a marked upturn in world opinion, but our work rebuilding our image in the world is not yet done.

The second reason is because those of us on the left—including those of us who claim to support our president but do little to show it—need to step up to our narrative challenge in an intelligent and thoughtful way. Clearly the right, and the far right, do not have the answers we seek; they had eight years and a trillion or so dollars to figure it out and they failed. Nor should we fail to learn from the recent history that the right created. We need to urge lawmakers to pass laws that deal proactively with leaders who would take us to war under false or misleading information. Once such information is shown to be false or misleading, immediate impeachment proceedings should be triggered. And we should cooperate with any war crimes tribunals that The Hague might conduct, just as we now expect other nations to cooperate. It's too late to bring George W. Bush, Dick Cheney, and Donald Rumsfeld to justice in this country, but at least history will be their judge. What we can do is ensure that the future is not a repeat of the recent past, to truly learn from our history how best not to follow liars and fear-mongers into war.

To ensure that these sorts of crimes are not repeated, we must also be willing to engage those who continue to perpetrate and spread misleading statements in support of fear-mongering administrations from the media sidelines. For example, this is not the time to ignore the loudmouth Fox News commentator bashing health care reform as "socialism"; we must instead ask those under Shaytan's spell to define socialism. Because chances are good that he or she won't be able to do it. Not accurately. Or point out that the problem with President Obama is not that he is a secret socialist, but that he is perhaps too much a capitalist. He believes in private ownership of property, which is why he sponsored legislation to help citizens avoid foreclosure. He believes in private industry, thus his support of health care reform that values private insurance companies but offers a government mechanism for expanding coverage to those who cannot now afford private coverage. He bailed out the banks. Sigh. No, our president is not a socialist. He is a *progressive* who inherited one hell of mess. He's not perfect. But he represents the best chance we have to articulate a vision for America that inspires trust abroad and hope at home.

We cannot change the image of the U.S. military as Crusaders in Iraq and Afghanistan by simply turning into anti-Crusaders at home. Our opposition to war must be tempered by political and ethical realities. What we inherited was a mismanaged political mess, but it is *still our responsibility*, our moral and ethical responsibility. We should not simply abandon our mission in the region, which would be, in effect, to condemn those who live there to further tyranny and oppression, warfare and violence. To do that would be to sentence *ourselves* to further menace in the long run. To do that would be to turn our narrative promise, the promise we offer the world, into hypocrisy. Instead, we must, as President Obama has articulated it, embrace the duality of war and peace, find better ways of engaging war to make peace, *while making it central to the narrative that peace is always the end goal*, and not be deterred by extremists near and far who do not share our cause.

We need the left to engage in the war. Both the near war and the far war. To achieve peace requires challenging extremists at home and abroad. To be successful in that challenge requires both our participation and our leadership.

5. The Academic Dilemma
Higher Education as a Battleground in the War of Ideas

In this chapter I offer a brief critique of the politics threatening higher education in an age of political extremism. It is a political extremism at home that threatens to end not just the beautiful dream I once had, but more importantly, it threatens to destroy the dreams our students have, and will continue to have, for the foreseeable future.

Fair warning: this chapter could have been an entire book. Certainly the topic of education reform and the politics of funding deserve more of an in-depth treatment than I provide here, but my goal is not to provide a comprehensive critique.[1] Nor is it to join in the far-left chorus that sees the entrepreneurial university as a co-opted corporate state that rails against "cognitive capitalism" and views faculty as conscripted labor in a "knowledge-for-profit" enterprise that ultimately threatens academic freedom and civil rights.[2] For as is the case with the far-left and the war, the far-left and the academy suffer from a reductionist stereotype that equates "critique" with lockstep ideologically-driven Marxist thought permeated by an existential gloom, elite conspiracies, and the end game of power. Because of this stereotype—and despite the fact that the far-left critique of the academy offers legitimate insights and some good reasons for being nervous—progressives in the academy are often tarred with the same broad Marxist brush. The result has been singularly devastating. And meanwhile, in state legislatures and capitol buildings, the far-right rhetoric reigns.

My goal is to show how a particular variety of extremist narrative—the hypocrite, or traitor narrative—reveals a sinister dimension to education politics on the far right. Using those strong terms may shock you, but bear with me. There is a lot at stake here for those of us who have dedicated our lives to education. For anyone with children. And for our country. For this reason I provide a series of observations that may at first seem disconnected, but bear with me. By the end of the chapter you will understand that not only do these seemingly disparate issues contribute themes to a common extremist narrative, but that the narrative itself must be taken very seriously—and actively countered—by all of us.

When I entered college in the fall of 1970, Richard Milhous Nixon was president of the United States and there was a war in Vietnam. I felt privileged to be in college. I would become the first person in my family to graduate from a four-year school, something my father had been unable to do because WWII interrupted his studies, and something my mother had been unable to do because I, their only child, had been born.

For many students "going to college" was a parental dream fulfilled. A college education separated those of us who would wear suits and skirts from those of us whose choice of occupation was based on the answer one gave to this critical question: "Do you prefer to work indoors or outdoors?" A college degree is what separated managers, professionals, and leaders from workers and employees. It was the higher cultural passageway that led us into adulthood armed with knowledge gained from applying our minds to the liberal arts and sciences; with skill in using language, both in writing and in speech; and with an abiding cultural and political confidence that—we hoped—transcended divisions of race, class, and gender. Then, with degree in hand, it would be our turn to make the world better.

We were up for the challenge. College was hard work but we expected it also to be a fun place. We'd seen the movies and read the novels. We'd heard the stories from older siblings and parents. We expected our weekends to be filled with social activities, football games, and fraternity/sorority parties. We would have friends from around the world, or at least from out of state. We would be living away from home, expressing our independence, testing our limits. There might well be sex. We could fall in love. We would discover our passion as well as our way into the adult world. Somewhere along the way, someone would hand over that secret decoder ring and suddenly everything would make sense.

Real professors would teach us. They would impart the deep structures of history, philosophy, science, literature, and art that would illuminate the world. Professors would also advise us. They would see into those hidden dimensions of our character and talent and offer us new ways of thinking about ourselves, about who we were and what we could do. They would challenge our ideas, debate with us the merits of this or that, provide us with the intellectual equipment we lacked, and offer us new questions to think about and new methods for thinking about them. When we graduated, some four years hence, we would enter a job market that welcomed us, or go on to some postgraduate school. "Going to college" would be replaced by "college graduate," and once again our parents would smile because the life such a label offered, the opportunities it promised, were so much better than what they had inherited from their folks. It would then be our turn to work for an even better world to hand over to our own children. This romantic vision was part and parcel of the progressive liberal narrative. Of an archetypal American story, one part Horatio Alger and one part happily ever after film script. We had read the books and seen the movies; now we wanted *the life*.

Judging from talks I have had over the years with parents and entering freshmen, that imagined and highly romantic idealized version of college life and the entitled life after college hasn't changed very much. For many citizens, "going to college" is still a major achievement and graduation from college is viewed as a ticket to a better life. While those dreams haven't changed, the realities of college life have changed a great deal.

It's not a mystery why that change has occurred; all you have to do to begin to unravel the difference between then and now is follow the money and link it to an accompanying conservative narrative that has become increasingly extremist. That conservative narrative, which, for argument's sake, I am going to say began in the modern era with the publication in 1951 of *God and Man at Yale* by William Buckley, presents readers with a view of college life that is less about learning the higher truth than it is about being indoctrinated into lower leftist, and, for Catholic Buckley, Godless politics. The idea of a college educated woman or man was made suspect, a trend that continued apace in conservative thought for decades defined by "the culture wars" and that is still with us today.[3] So it is that in 2010 the conservative view that posits a college education as something that right-minded parents ought to fear because their well-mannered right-thinking children will be exposed to radical, left-wing, Marxist, social justice, and feminist ideas is still with us. In that way, the 1960s culture wars never ended.

As the conservative narrative gained momentum, a new metaphor was introduced that forever altered how legislative bodies and senior administrators thought about what a college was really all about. That metaphor was "the entrepreneurial" or "business" model that equated universities with factories organized to produce inventions, patents, grants, contracts, and marketable ideas.[4] Today college presidents and senior administrators seldom question the metaphor and its accompanying narrative, because without the additional capital provided by these external resources, their institutions—and particularly large state universities—would be broke. Furthermore, administrators and college presidents are also politicians. They campaign for career moves upward in institutions where success is equated with increased revenues under their watch. There is every good reason for them to buy into the entrepreneurial model and to invest in those areas under their purview that generate resources.

The entrepreneurial model does not entirely eliminate the need for state support, but it does mean that seeing the advantages of decreased spending on universities, state legislatures have generally accepted the conservative narrative on funding. They, too, pretty much roundly believe that the proper business of education is business. They see universities not as protected cultural spaces for the advancement of learning (which sounds vaguely leftist anyway), but as incubators for new ways to advance the state's economy.

On the upside, the entrepreneurial university has tied its success to more jobs, new industries, financial growth, and a host of other positive attributes contributing to a state economy. On the downside, as state institutions of higher learning generate more and more revenue, conservative legislators view it as an opportunity to lessen the burden on taxpayers—always their mantra—because, in their view, universities no longer need state governments for financial support. Hence, conservatives who campaign for education reform (e.g., throw out liberal ideas and cut waste), and who want their universities to be "the best in the world" (e.g. the best entrepreneurs in the world), also tend to campaign on tax relief because they understand these ideas to be intricately connected as well as right minded. In every sense of the word.

But looked at differently, when the funding model changes, so, too, does college.

In 1970, the year I entered college, I could have gone to the University of Pennsylvania or to Shepherd College. In retrospect those two diverse schools represent totally different educational experiences, but at the time I was basing my selection of college on entirely personal things. I had lived in Philadelphia through most of my high school years and thought I might want to go back there. Or I could go to Shepherd in West Virginia, where my girlfriend was going and where her dad was a dean.

Money had little to do with it. The annual tuition and fees to enter the elite University of Pennsylvania were $2,450.[5] As an out-of-state student at Shepherd College, my tuition and fees were only slightly less at $2,250. I had scholarship money that could be used anywhere. I chose Shepherd for all the wrong reasons. By the end of my first month there my girlfriend dumped me and transferred to another school, and my relationship with her dad, the dean, was never the same. Nevertheless, I did well at Shepherd, graduated in 1973, made my parents proud, and remember my time there fondly.

Years pass as years do, quickly and then more quickly. I moved through the next thirty-seven years of my life on many college

campuses like a man in a hurry, or so it now seems. I made a career as
a teacher/scholar/administrator. I lived through the methods wars in
my own discipline and the culture wars across the whole of campuses.
I gained a somewhat bifurcated perspective on higher education and
higher education institutions, one informed by my continuous role as
a faculty member and the other by my experiences as a department
chair of a small unit, as a department head of a multi-disciplinary
unit, and as director of a large and diverse school of communication.
I came to understand that the two perspectives were often at odds
with each other. But I learned from both of them and am comfortable
with the skill set I've developed as a result. I have lived the "entrepreneurial life," created successful "strategic initiatives" designed to apply
communication research to real world problems with the anticipa-
tion of generating new revenues, and participated in a wide range of
activities—from high-end fund raisers to the creation of online courses and degree completion programs for the business community. I
trot out these accomplishments because I think it is important for
you to know that about me as you read through the next few pages.

Now back to the money. Remember, it *is* about the money.

In 2010, Penn charged $38,000 for tuition and fees; Shepherd
University charged $10,695 for out-of-state students, $6,525 for in-
state. Even discounting inflation differences, the change in tuition
is startling. For example, Shepherd's $2,250 cost in 1970 dollars
equals $13,137 today, which would indicate that Shepherd is doing
an excellent job of actually *reducing* the cost of education, whereas
the University of Pennsylvania is not ($2,450 in 1970 equals $14,304 in
2010). That comparison, of course, does not tell the whole story.

The University of Pennsylvania is a private institution. It does
not receive financial support from the state of Pennsylvania. Nor is it
bound by any state mandate to keep the cost of tuition low. Nor does
it serve the same economically and socially diverse population as a
typical state school. It also is located in the city of Philadelphia, where
the cost of everything related to construction and maintenance of
facilities, as well as the cost of living in general, is considerably higher than it is in Shepherdstown, West Virginia. So while it may seem
that Penn is gouging its students, really it is not. In fact, as is the case
with most elite institutions, Penn offers the majority of students—60

percent in 2010—financial grant aid, thereby significantly reducing their tuition bills.

Although elite institutions have suffered during the current economic downturn, I am not worried overly much about them. If they had deep pockets before this mess started, they will survive. More worrying to me is *the declining support for higher education provided by states* to state institutions.[6] Beneath that italicized subordinate clause lies a far darker story. It's a political story, one that features archetypal hypocrites and traitors engaged in a war of ideas against ordinary citizens and educators, and, although I'm not fond of conspiracy theories, there is a conspiracy in it.

Allow me to begin with a personal example. I currently teach at Arizona State University (ASU), which is as of this writing the largest campus in America. We have approximately 65,000 students. In 2009 our tuition for in-state students was among the lowest in the United States ($5,500), and we provide tuition assistance in the form of grants, scholarships, and work-study options to approximately 70 percent of our undergraduates. Despite our conservative tuition revenues, when the current economic crisis hit the state of Arizona, the first thing our Republican-dominated legislature did was to cut our budget by $100 million in addition to the $100 million they had already cut the year before.

One result of those cuts was that state support for students was reduced to the same level as in 1980.[7] Another was the termination of 950 staff positions and 250 lecturers. All faculty were required to take "furloughs," which meant that we were simply not paid for up to fifteen days of work, depending on salary level. On those "days off at no pay" we were strictly forbidden to do any ASU-related work or even to use ASU equipment (such as computers or email), but many of us found that such an arrangement, while technically legal, was in practice impossible. We still had the same work to do, regardless of whether or not we were getting paid. In addition, some departments were combined and some colleges were "disestablished" to save administrative costs. And while we were engaged in downsizing our faculty, staff, salaries, and facilities, the state of Arizona insisted that we enroll more and more students. In fact, our funding formula is directly related to the increase in the number of enrolled freshman annually—it is the only mechanism for determining what the state contributes to the university.

Arizona is somewhat unusual in that the economic crisis created by "the bubble" in our housing industry was one of the worst in the country. We are also crippled by a Republican state legislature that is largely unwilling to raise taxes in order to support higher education, and more than a few legislators who are openly hostile to funding education at all. Other states are in similar straits—from Florida to California, from Nevada to Missouri, from Illinois to Pennsylvania— and the stories there are much the same as our story: teachers are fired; class sizes are doubled; no new resources are allocated for buildings, equipment, or supplies; and the idea that states are required to provide an education for their citizens is openly and sometimes vehemently under attack. For example, in Florida, until courageous Governor Charlie Crist refused to sign a draconian education reform bill, tenure in K-12 Florida schools would have been abolished and teacher pay tied solely to student performance on one end-of-the-year standardized test. There would be no extra pay given to teachers with masters or doctoral degrees. That this draconian bill passed the legislature despite widespread protest is indicative of the general attitude the majority of Republicans, and everyone on the far-right, holds toward education. Simply put, they don't believe that public support for education is important.

Yet they want their children educated. Herein lies the paradox of education in these United States. I used to think education was unique in this regard, but I was wrong. Since the Tea Party movement gained momentum, I have come to view the paradox at the heart of what Republicans and Teabaggers want differently. But it took Bill Maher to pull it together for me. He says:

> The problem with the tea party movement ... is that they want money for nothing and chicks for free. They want a deregulated free market and their jobs to stay here in the U.S.; they want guaranteed health coverage regardless of preexisting conditions without a big government mandate; they want to call themselves

teabaggers and people to keep a straight face. And of course they want big tax cuts along with deficit reduction. I can't even think of a suitable analogy for that disconnect—it's like thinking getting a handjob will clean your garage.[8]

Education is just part of a far more general, and more troubling, attitude. Viewed alongside the other funding paradoxes, we see a fundamental lunacy that cuts across all government-run programs. No wonder Marc Ambinder, the political editor for the *Atlantic Monthly*, was pressed to ask, "Have the conservatives gone mad?"[9]

It would seem so. Not only have they abandoned reason when it comes to demanding the government provide services without supporting them with new revenues—or even with existing revenues—they have also singularly failed to bring into the discussion any serious consideration of the *defense budget*. That budget by far accounts for where most of our taxes go, a sum that is greater than defense spending *by the next fifteen countries*. If conservatives, Republicans, and especially Teabaggers were serious about questioning the efficiency of government-run programs, they would look to defense spending first. Once again, Bill Maher:

> Everything that goes into defense costs us about a trillion dollars a year, most of which goes into fighting the Russians in 1978. Fighter planes for all those dog fights we get into with the Taliban, submarines to foil their evil plot to blow up our ships with car bombs, and space lasers to shoot down their exploding underpants...scream about handouts, this is what they should be protesting.[10]

Of course included in Maher's criticism are serious questions about defense spending under the Obama administration. Maher is on the left, and some would say—I would agree with them—the far left, so why does it fall to liberals—including far lefties—to do the critical work that conservatives should be doing? I'm not talking about talking heads or radio pundits or former circus clowns, but thoughtful conservatives? This same point was also underscored by Ambinder:

> Can anyone deny that the most trenchant and effective criticism of President Obama today comes not from the right but from the left? Rachel Maddow's grilling of administration economic

officials. Keith Olbermann's hectoring of Democratic leaders on the public option. Glenn Greenwald's criticisms of Elena Kagan. Ezra Klein and Jonathan Cohn's keepin'-them-honest perspectives on health care. The civil libertarian left on detainees and Gitmo. The *Huffington Post* on derivatives.[11]

To say nothing of liberal academics, gay rights advocates, immigration reform leaders, and those of us who oppose the war. From President Obama's perspective, perhaps with friends like us, who needs Teabaggers? Or Republicans?

One hallmark of liberal thought is that, unlike conservatives, we tend to eat our own. We openly contradict our leaders. We can't help it. Organized and energized by the belief that people should be held accountable for their promises and policies, we are the Lexus of American politics: relentless in our pursuit of perfection. We hold our politicians to higher political standards. We expect them to use the same powers of passion and reason that guided them to victory during the campaign to characterize their follow-through actions once in office. We lose faith in them if they fail us. And that, unfortunately, is our liberal Achilles heel.

By contrast, our enemies on the right and especially the far right are notoriously proud for refusing to back down when caught in contradictions or even outright lies. For example, Karl Rove's memoir *Courage and Consequences* essentially rewrites a history of the Bush administration from the unrepentant victor's perspective. It is a large lie told without hesitation or remorse. Brushing aside the complete misleading of the American public about WMDs in Iraq and the complete mess that followed Bush declaring "victory" on an aircraft carrier in one of the most staged propaganda performances of our time, Rove admits only that he ought to have defended the president with more vigor. He assesses President Bush's reign—and one can only assume his role in creating and perpetrating it—on the last page of the book, thusly: "[Our] achievements over eight years were impressive, durable and significant."[12]

They certainly were that. What was "impressive" is that this administration's deregulation policies and failure to raises taxes to pay for two costly wars nearly brought down America's economic system as well as almost bankrupted the world. What is "durable" are the home foreclosures and job losses that will be with us for some time. And what was "significant" is that the Bush administration is getting away with it. Hardly a record to be proud of, Mr. Rove!

If it seems as if I have moved away from the education question, please understand that we in the education field are part of a much larger plot against America being perpetrated by the right. That is why the argument I cast here is made of a broader net. For, my friends, this is not a conspiracy of dumb-asses against liberals alone. *It is a conspiracy to undermine the ideal of democratic citizenship championed by the Founding Fathers: an informed electorate.* And the people responsible for it should be labeled for what they are: hypocrites and traitors.

I understand fully that those on the far right want to control the information that is given to students; hence, the Texas textbook fight. If you control the textbooks, you have twelve years to narrow what counts as "truth" from a diversity of voices to one voice that is shaped by two forces: (1) an evangelical Christian intolerance, and (2) a belief that the most valuable education—from elementary school through college—is directly related to "pre-professional" job training. For these folks, the purpose of an education is not to enlighten the mind or to discover new ideas or to challenge existing wisdom. It is to prepare young people for a lifetime of obedient work in a Christian version of America, Inc.

Allow me to explain. The evangelical Christian intolerance for anything or anyone who challenges the authority of the literal Bible is a sweeping intellectual category. It includes most science and scientists (think: evolutionary biology, stem cell research, and theoretical physicists, especially); most of the humanities but especially history, literature, and philosophy (all leftist disciplines, by their account); all social sciences, but especially justice studies, sociology, psychology, and communication studies (because we emphasize knowledge of the secular); the arts, for obvious reasons; and of course, all "area studies," but especially those dedicated to race and gender. What this strategy—if successful—would accomplish is the systemic removal of

critical thinking as well as any program of study that includes advocacy aimed at challenging the authority of received, Biblical wisdom. It
would help to produce a nation of citizens who do what they are told
to do, preferably by a right-minded leader who professes the "one true
faith," such as George W. Bush, Sarah Palin, or perhaps Mitt Romney.
It would remake public colleges and universities on the model of, say,
Liberty University.

The belief that most higher education should be reduced to pre-
professional job training is evident when patterns of private gifts to
public universities are examined. Look at your own school. Where
does conservative money go? What do they invest in? The overwhelming answer at ASU is to schools of business and engineering.
And from reports I've received from colleagues around the country,
ASU's experience is not unique. Of course conservatives, like liberals and moderates, are free to give their money to whomever they
choose, so my objection is less about their freedom to do exactly that
and more about what "comes with" it.

For example, Bruce Spock recently investigated the increasingly
dependent role of public universities on private giving. He reports that
it "shapes the university in ways that challenge academic traditions."[13]
And what might those changes be? One change is to unbalance the
power that used to be held by the humanities, sciences, and social sciences in favor of departments and schools (such as business and engineering) that either ignore or discount the intellectual contributions of
the humanities and social sciences by de-emphasizing or limiting the
number of hours their majors are required to spend in them.

This preference for a pre-professional job training template also
has negative impacts on how academic research—and therefore,
faculty—is evaluated. The favored disciplines are decidedly quantitative and so, too, is the evaluation standard. The favored metric for
evaluating scholarly work is derived from four measures: (a) the sheer
number of articles and books published during an academic year; (b)
the number of citations for a study in peer reviewed journals; (c) the
impact rating of the journal; and (d) the dollar amount of external
investments in a faculty member's research program.

If the conservative challenge to academic culture was limited
to evaluation metrics that favor traditional quantitative work over

critical-cultural pedagogy, or qualitative studies in general, it would be bad enough. After all, much critical-cultural work and most ethnography, already devalued by a general lack of federal grant support, has been further marginalized by a lack of sheer volume of studies published by single authors in a given year as well as by the fact that the story form used for narrative inquiry often doesn't include citations, and the journals that feature qualitative work are often not ranked as highly as their more traditional, quantitative brethren. This pattern of bias against qualitative research is also found in new regulations and guidelines for conducting and evaluating research in the United Kingdom[14] and in Australia.[15]

Under the Bush administration in America, and similar conservative governments around the globe, the far-right challenge to academic scholarship became much worse. As Norman K. Denzin and Michael D. Giardina put it, "Around the globe governments are attempting to regulate scientific inquiry by defining what is good science."[16] And increasingly, "good science" is defined as that which supports a far-right conservative agenda. This means research that "(1) has the appearance of being factual; (2) it is patriotic; and (3) it supports a political action that advances ... the far-right neoconservative agenda."[17] This politically-motivated model for assessing the worth of academic research drove funding for the No Child Left Behind act and the attempts to undermine the science behind "global warming" under President Bush.[18]

It is a case of the money—on a business model that expects measurable returns on investments—driving the engines of change throughout academic culture. But at what cost?

As recorded history and personal experience teaches us all: with money comes power, and with power often comes undue influence on what is considered important or vital to the interests of those in power. As university presidents, provosts, and deans struggle to find adequate resources in these tough economic times, gifts from alumni and friends often make big differences, not only in sustaining programs, faculty, and curricula, but moreover in determining future directions for the institution.

For example, when elite new programs named for wealthy donors are launched, they often come with elite new faculty and money for everything from equipment to staff. But investors are smart. They seldom give money without at least a few strings attached. And one of those strings is usually that the university has to "match" certain of the donated funds, generally in the area reserved for providing instruction, and support for that instruction, in classes. The more generous the gift, the more the donor usually requires from the institution. And, the institution knows it is in its longer-term best interests to find a way to make the donor happy. Why? Because the likelihood of more money coming from the same donor a few years down the road depends on it.

Money that goes into one account means that same money isn't put into another account, or accounts. When severe budget cuts come—as they have since we entered this global economic downturn—hard decisions about programs, faculty, and staff have to be made. And when this happens, even the ablest administrators tend to protect two things: core curriculum and donor-derived programs. Schools and departments that generate their own revenues (from number of majors that generate tuition dollars to grants to online offerings) and/or have their own donors tend to be favored over schools and departments that have neither. In matters of money, money matters. Once again, although it may be painful for you to contemplate, think about your own institution during this time of economic trouble and consider who and what is finally left standing.

It didn't used to be this way, at least for public colleges and universities. There are, of course, many reasons for the shift away from public financing of higher education to what is called the "entrepreneurial model" that transfers fiscal responsibility from the state to the institution. One reason is obvious. Since the age of Reagan the public, which is to say the electorate, has been brainwashed into believing that waste is everywhere in government programs, taxes are bad regardless of what those revenues support, and the outright lie that education in America has failed in its mission.[19]

Collectively these political claims have had a devastating impact on higher education funding models, particularly in conservative states where state legislators and governors claim to be in favor of education but routinely vote against funding increases or new taxes to support it. When combined with a propagandistic never-ending campaign narrative about "failed schools" (referring to K-12) that ignores the root sociological and political bases for low performing students in under-funded districts as well as in middle class suburbs, the result is a general lack of public confidence in education writ large that continues to feed, if not warrant, the hypocrisy.[20]

Where did we go wrong? When did we decide that public education was something we shouldn't pay for? Or that unequal funding for school districts based on property taxes was okay? David R. Jones writes that the root of the public school funding problem was

> a 1973 Supreme Court 5-4 decision in San Antonio Independent School District v. Rodriguez (No. 71-1332 Supreme Court of the United States, 411 U.S. 1; 93 S. Ct. 1278), which held that reliance on property taxes to fund public schools does not violate the Equal Protection Clause of the Fourteenth Amendment to the U.S. Constitution, even if it causes inter-district expenditure disparities.
>
> The decision basically allows the United States to be virtually alone in the developed world to allow public education funding to rely on how wealthy your community is rather than providing an equal allocation of funding for each child. Thurgood Marshall wrote one of his strongest dissents, which in hindsight captures just how far we went wrong: "The majority's holding can only be seen as a retreat from our historic commitment to equality of educational opportunity."[21]

Again we confront the hypocrisy of saying one thing—"I support education; our schools must be among the best in the nation"—and acting on that campaign promise by either doing nothing at all to address the root causes of poor performance or by cutting financial support for education by cutting back on those property taxes.

The right's answer to disparities in funding are (1) vouchers, which would rob already stretched public school budgets while propping up church-based schools; (2) charter schools, which have largely proven to be failures; and (3) advertising campaigns based on catchy slogans, such as "No Child Left Behind," which do nothing to address the root causes but ensure that many children will be, in fact, left behind. Lately, however, the right's turn against public education has become more pronounced. Far right legislators have suggested in Arizona, Florida, California, Missouri, and elsewhere that the state government should get out of the education business entirely.

Please don't misunderstand my position. You know and I know schools need reform. There are bad schools and bad teachers. And I think President Obama's "Race to the Top" initiative is correct in its assessment that what is needed to reform schools includes raising academic standards, requiring rigorous student testing, calling for more teacher evaluation and training, and demanding accountability. But I do not believe that reforming schools is the same thing as addressing the root sociological and political bases of the problems faced by students who are raised in families that do not value education; by one or more parents who do not read to them or help with school work; who live in neighborhoods that are neither safe nor secure; and who often suffer from a lack of nutrition, a lack of exercise, and who rely on a television or video game for companionship; children who are abused and neglected; children who must work to support their family; plus a host of other problems that schools are not designed to solve and that programs such as these are unable to address.

That said, one problem that could be addressed is funding. This is not simply a case of asking the public to throw good money after bad, but instead to recognize that not funding public education won't solve the problem. How could it? Instead, what is needed is a renewed commitment to public education, both in word and deed. This means that when politicians on either side of the aisle claim to want the best schools, hold them to it. Get them to go into detail on how they plan to accomplish that goal, including how they plan to secure the revenues necessary to carry out any new plan or campaign.

For too long America has expected too much and contributed too little to education at all levels. States that have managed to keep their commitments to education have created the strongest economic engines for their people, because an educated workforce, excellent schools, and affordable, high quality educational opportunities for employees attract new businesses. The former chancellor of the University of North Carolina system, William Friday, when challenged as to why in hard economic times he was firmly against budget cuts to higher education, once put it this way: "If you want to know what the value of higher education is to the economy of a state, just compare North Carolina to South Carolina."

I was recently at a small gathering of friends and the topic of budget cuts to schools in Arizona came up in conversation. A fellow I had just met told us that his company was forced to pay a premium to get top employees to move to Phoenix. "Why is that," I asked? His was a sad smile. "Because the schools are not as good as they are at home, and our human resources office recommends private over public schools for our kids. The premium is enough to cover their tuition."

It's not just Arizona. And it's got to stop. The future of America requires a highly educated workforce to compete in a global economy against nations who do value education. It's that simple. If we can afford to bail out the banks, we can afford to improve our schools, pay our teachers, and invest in research and teaching that move all of us forward.

Among the studies in *Master Narratives of Islamist Extremists* is one that the other authors and I call "the hypocrites" that shows a marked similarity to these strategic moves. We identify both Hebrew (the supposedly devout Hebrews who built a sacred cow once Moses went up the mountain) and Muslim (*al-Munafiqin*, in *Sura 63*) antecedents to modern hypocrites, described thusly:

> The imposters, or "hypocrites," are insincere insiders who go along with the group when it benefits them, but are quick to disrupt it for their own benefit when it suits them. They can appear outwardly to be the most pious in the community, as if wearing righteous masks, but when Moses goes up the mountain, or they retreat behind the closed doors of Medina, or into the

secret recesses of their hearts, there is no sincerity in their faith or actions. Thus the hypocrite is a danger to the true believers unlike any other because they represent a profound danger within the group. For Islamist extremists, the Hypocrites narrative fits perfectly into their struggles against their fellow [apostate or non-true believer] Muslims, or the so-called "near enemy."[22]

Our "near enemy" operates in much the same way. They are right-wing politicians but they are also voters on the right who claim to believe in education but vote against it. Our "near enemy" are hypocrites, and like those in the Old Testament and in the Qur'an, they represent a "profound danger" to America. Let us be honest: they are *traitors to democracy*.

The academic dilemma is what to do about it. Elsewhere in this book I point out that when I teach my class on Communication, Terrorism, and National Security I am careful not to reveal my personal politics. Given the tone of this book some of you may find that claim hard to believe, but there it is. Although I respect the right of my colleagues who do so to wear their politics openly and to give fair warning to students on the first day of class about how their political commitments influence how they see and interpret their subjects, I am more old-school. I seek out strong arguments from both sides of the many issues that emanate from my subject matter. I believe education is about opening minds to contrary points of view as well as providing them with tools to analyze those points of view. In the spirit of Kenneth Burke, I consider theories to be "equipment for living."

So my academic dilemma is personal as well as professional. How do I reconcile my liberal politics these days with my professional commitment to a practiced, definitely staged, neutrality? Probably some of you are asking the same question. For me it is also a question that is entirely pragmatic, given the educational ends I hope to achieve. Nothing turns away students faster than far-left cant or rant. They aren't paying tuition to hear replays of Olbermann vs. O'Reilly. They are here to learn what questions to ask, how to parse the daily dose of marketing and propaganda that permeate their lives. They are here to find out what they can take with them when they leave, what they can put to use to build lives, careers, and communities.

So what do I do?

Because my subject is extremism in relation to the war of ideas since 9/11, I have learned to incorporate the rhetoric and narratives of the near enemy when discussing the rhetoric and narratives of the far enemy. I don't use narrative IEDs in the classroom, but I do discuss the concept in relation to tactics deployed by both sets of extremists. The results have been interesting. Most students come to class with very little knowledge of terrorism or the geographies of extremism, or the role of communication in those battles. They expect to hear me lecture and discuss issues related to Iraq, Afghanistan, Indonesia, Africa, even Europe. They do not expect me to discuss Michigan, or Arizona, or politicians in Washington, D.C. When students are exposed to the similarities (and differences) between extremists' narratives, uses of the Internet, recruitment strategies, and propaganda, they are at first uncomfortable but soon get over it.

I am careful to use both far-left and far-right extremist examples. Although this book has been purposefully designed to focus on the far-right, it would be foolish of me not to include examples drawn from eco-terrorists, People for the Ethical Treatment of Animals (PETA), anti-globalization groups worldwide, and others, including far-left academics, media commentators, and politicians. My point is that if we begin with the assumption, as I do, that communication creates our perceptions of reality, our identities, and our understanding of the world, then learning *how* communication achieves those ends is "equipment for living." I am far more convincing as a teacher when I expose both extremes, and that is precisely what I want to be: convincing.

I want my students to emerge from that class armed with intelligence about a topic that will be with us forever, because surely terrorism will never die. I also want them to be equipped with analytical tools to assess messages and to argue, but also I want them to use their knowledge and their skills when they decide how to vote. I believe in the democratic ideal of a well-informed citizen. As an academic, my job is to contribute significantly to that ideal. And as a scholar, as long as liberal education and democracy are under siege from the near enemy of hypocrites and traitors, my job is not to limit my discourse to traditional academic outlets, but to take what I have learned into the public sphere.

Where I hope to see you ...

In the meantime, what can you do to awaken students? What resources do you have to expose extremism, the politics of fear, the propaganda on television and the Internet? How can you promote social justice? What can you, we do to correct the destruction already done to our educational system? I don't have all of the answers, but I believe that working together, united by a progressive narrative about education and its value to the future of America, we can find them.

Change begins by challenging extremism at home. I urge you to use what you find in this book as a template for outlining the threat of extremism of all kinds, don't forget your obligation to present a fair and balanced view in your classes, and trust that the tools and knowledge you offer will improve the likelihood that your students will be inoculated against extremist rhetoric and that their inoculation will pay off in the next and all future elections.

6. Learning from Obama and Learning from Our Enemies

Steps toward a Progressive Core Narrative and Communication for the Common Good

There are hopeful signs in The Battle of Narratives. Health care reform passed into law. Student loan reform—and removing the big bad banks from the lending equation—passed into law. Reform of the financial industry is opening up new ways of thinking about the relationship of banks to communities and calling into question practices that reward greed over the common good. In the week following these announcements President Obama's approval rating jumped to 58 percent, and more and more people began admitting that reform of health care was a good thing. Implicit in these new laws and new questions and higher approval ratings is the fact that *the progressive ideal of using government to help people is a good idea.*

Leadership victory at home led to a major leadership victory abroad. On the international political scene, President Obama's victory in health care reform was quickly followed by a major success in reducing the nuclear threat to America:

> The new treaty with Russia, dubbed New START. . . verifiably reduces the threat posed by the only weapons that can destroy America. It shrinks, at least a little, the dangerously bloated U.S. and Russian nuclear stockpiles. But it does much more than that. It helps reset the relationship with Russia, whose cooperation is necessary for progress on Iran, the Middle East, global warming, European security and many other issues. But it does more than

137

that.... Now, he can move forward aggressively on agreements to lock up nuclear materials from terrorists, to stop new nations from getting these weapons, and to begin planning for a new round of negotiations to go from thousands of nuclear weapons to hundreds.[1]

Implicit in this landmark agreement is the idea that a muscular liberal narrative and a president who is not afraid to use it in foreign policy is a message the world has been waiting for. Planet Earth needs a strong America. For all our faults, we do stand for good things, and when good people are elected to high office we show our best political and moral face to the world. It is worth noting, also, that when Obama proposed reducing nuclear arsenals by one-third he was roundly criticized by Republicans and by pundits until it was pointed out to them—by Jon Stewart on the Daily Show, among others—that Obama's proposal was exactly that of Ronald Reagan in the 1980s.

Peter Beinard sees in these victories a new narrative strength in Obama that parallels that of Ronald Reagan, to wit:

> Will Obama become hugely popular anytime soon? Probably not. Reagan and the GOP still got clobbered in the 1982 midterm elections, largely because the country was in deep recession. And Obama and the Democrats will probably suffer this fall as well. But if the economy recovers in 2011 and 2012, and Obama rides that recovery to reelection, as Reagan did in 1984, he will be able to say he changed the rules of the political game, and won a mandate from the country. Then we'll know for sure what more and more people already suspect: The Age of Reagan is over. Welcome to the Age of Obama.[2]

Yet no sooner were these words released into the blogosphere than Obama announced his plan to begin drilling off the East Coast for oil, which in turn was followed by the tragic and unprecedented ecological destruction caused by the catastrophic BP oil leak in the Gulf of Mexico. In May, President Obama suspended offshore deepwater oil drilling, a decision that was overturned by a federal judge in June, followed by a rewrite by the Obama administration in July as a moratorium until the end of November. As of this last minute manuscript editing (August 2010) there has been no announcement from the White House of what will happen after the moratorium expires, although that announcement is expected sometime in late September.

This plan for a moratorium rather than the pursuit of an outright ban upset many liberals as well as many supporters of continued deep-water drilling. The idea, according to Michael Bromwich, the newly appointed director of the Bureau of Ocean Energy Management, Regulation and Enforcement, was to have enough time to draft new safety regulations and disaster recovery plans—a clear sign that Obama intends to reopen offshore deepwater drilling rather than ban it. Clearly, Obama's intention runs contrary to most progressives' ideas about the matter, preferring, as he does, to use government as a partner to enterprise, but a partner who relies on laws and regulations to protect us, to enable innovation, and to promote responsible prosperity rather than to shut it down. This pragmatic stance creates problems for liberals, as Eric Alterman puts it:

> Liberals were all set to paint Obama as "their Reagan." But this is deeply misguided. Yes, deep down he's a liberal, but an intensely pragmatic one. As David Remnick demonstrates in his master-ful new biography, *The Bridge*, Obama is unlikely to hold on to deeply ideological views with a goal of reordering American politics from top to bottom. He prefers to take what's on the table.[3]

This is exactly the point. President Obama is a *pragmatic* progressive. He is not, and never will be, a doctrinaire liberal. As a result he maintains a core narrative that warrants the use of government to improve lives and protect our security, but on issues as far-ranging as nuclear energy, offshore drilling, and the wars in Iraq and Afghanistan, he complicates that narrative to accomplish strategic *longer*-term goals that are in the long term best interest of the country and indeed the world.

From a communication perspective, Obama's counter-narrative strategy is one we should all study. It is an intriguing combination of Lakoffian reframing mixed with an ability to turn binary oppositions into dialectical tensions. He uses humor as well as gentle ridicule and humiliation to augment logical reasoning. He is a master of the personal narrative as evidence of suffering, of need, and of pain that can only be alleviated by government assistance and political leadership.

He focuses almost exclusively on what will be, and on where we want to go, not on what has been. And he is articulate. He embodies the Ciceronian ideal of "the good man speaking well."

Between the time of this writing and the midterm elections I am confident that other good laws will be passed and other good things will occur because of President Obama's leadership. After those results are in, who knows? And this is why I have to repeat this mantra one more time: *he cannot do it alone.* Pragmatic progress requires *our* participation—our narrative participation—and that participation requires not ignoring the enemies at the front and back doors of our nation. They call for our blood. We must challenge them and their hatred with a better counter-narrative.

Extremists are our real enemies, not President Obama. We won't agree with everything he advances—I don't—but consider the other side's endorsement of extremist midterm candidates, continued tax cuts for the rich (despite the deficit), the threatened repeal of health care reform, further deep cuts to education and social services, the threat Mitch McConnell and others pose to the Fourteenth Amendment, the general assault on reason and justice, and it should become quite clear that Obama's continued success in creating reform remains our country's best hope for a progressive future.

Yet Obama and all progressives are under siege daily from those extremists who would "take back" our country with their twisted "Hatriot" narrative and whose whisperings via extremist media outlets have infected mainstream conservatives and most of the Republican party. While we on the left have been quietly bitching among ourselves about Obama's unwillingness to embrace strictly liberal policies, and while we have been collectively wishing Democrats in Congress would grow some cojones and get into the fight, the right has used our relative rhetorical inaction and perceived narrative weakness to successfully launch a widespread propaganda campaign to not only reduce the president's popularity (down from 58 percent in February to 44 percent in mid-August), but moreover to attack the rightful role of good government in promoting the values we hold most dear:

equality under the law, justice for all, an affordable quality education for everyone, and the right of a free and democratic people to be protected from corporate greed and political corruption.

Their storyline—well sharpened after thirty years of practice—begins with a binary conflict between those who believe that a strong government is a good thing and those who oppose it on the grounds that it interferes with our freedom as a people to attain the American Dream. The plot thickens with ideological assumptions—most of them without real evidence and with a good deal of history and experience to the contrary—that left to our own devices, conservative people, corporations, and small businesses will do the right thing. It further posits—again, against experience or evidence—that we don't need government regulations because they represent unnecessary "red tape" that gets in the way of the pursuit of profits. Disasters that result from a lack of regulation—say, the BP oil leak—are explained away, as Sarah Palin did, as the fault of overzealous environmentalists perpetrating a con and who are also probably not true Americans. "Radical environmentalists: you are damaging the planet with your efforts to lock up safer drilling areas. There's nothing clean and green about your misguided, nonsensical radicalism, and Americans are on to you as we question your true motives."[4]

The extremist storyline continues its ideological ascent by borrowing a principle from the Libertarian gospel. It asserts that we don't need government taxing us because taxes rob us of the right we have as free citizens to spend our money any way we choose. After all, it is our money. This is a free country. And we certainly don't need or want government to use our tax dollars to "redistribute the wealth" (implying, cynically, that using taxes to improve the opportunities of the less fortunate or privileged is really just a liberal excuse to gain votes from those who are too lazy, too stupid, or too different to figure out how to get their own piece of the American pie, and is, therefore, contrary to true-blue American values). Accordingly, the storyline includes but seldom articulates openly that those who adhere to it don't really approve of people who espouse beliefs different from what "we" take to be "mainstream." Nor do they want to support—and about these issues they are open and vocal—scientists who question God's word in the Holy Bible or those who promote stem cell research; liberal college professors (which we know means *all* college professors) who teach critical thinking to "our" children and therefore arm them with embarrassing questions about what "we" want to continue to believe to be true; or, as if the streets of mainstream America are heavily populated by them, those crazy socialists and Communists who want to take what "we" have earned and give it to someone else. Their storyline climaxes, always, with a crescendo of flag-draped patriotic fervor: We are a freedom loving people and this is the best country on Earth. God Bless America!

The rhetorical charm of this storyline—aside from its ideological biases or fictional qualities—is that it so smoothly supports the extremist master narrative: that our country is under siege and has been taken over by socialists/Communists/Nazis (Obama and those who voted for him), and it is the duty of all patriotic Americans to "take back the country," reestablish the Reagan Caliphate, and end once and for all that misguided Jeffersonian notion of the separation of church and state. Only then will freedom ring from sea to shining sea. Only then will the evil, corrupting influences of liberal media, college professors, and others of their ilk be vanquished from the land. Only then will America be America as the founding fathers intended.

So, my progressive friend, what do you say to all that? What, indeed, *should* we say in response to all that? Because we need to be actively involved in engaging—and countering—that infectious master narrative and its nonsensical supporting storyline. We cannot expect our president, or even our leaders, to carry the narrative ball on every play.

A *core* counter-narrative is what we lack. Until we have one that works as well as theirs, we risk losing The Battle of Narratives, and with it, the elections of 2010 and 2012. Crafting that core progressive narrative must be our communication mission for the foreseeable future.

Part of our core narrative challenge is to convince people to take a view of our problems, our politics, and our solutions that goes *beyond a single election cycle*. For example, there is an organization called The Long Now, run by Stewart Brand, that focuses on setting goals for the next *10,000 years* (http://www.longnow.org/). By looking far, far into the future, Brand and his colleagues hope to move beyond the politics and petty self-interests that govern thinking focused on the present and the near-future. The guidelines listed on the Long Now website for creating long-lived and long-valuable institutions mirror those embodied in President Obama's agenda. They are:

* Serve the long view
* Foster responsibility
* Reward patience
* Mind mythic depth
* Ally with competition
* Take no sides
* Leverage longevity

There is a lot to be gained in the short run from adopting the view that we are responsible for both the short term now *and* the long term future. If we, the progressives, projected our causes, our mission, and our proposed solutions against long term outcomes, we could foster real and sustainable change not just for our children, or our children's children, but for *generations* to come. That longer term aim should be part of how we frame our progressive narrative.

Second, following President Obama's example, we should build into our narrative an appreciation and a role for those whose political and/or religious orientations differ from ours, but who contribute to the common good and to the longer view afforded by a progressive vision. For example, some individuals on the right who are generally identified with religion are speaking out against religious extremism. CNN recently reported that a coalition of one hundred leading Christians, from Jim Wallis on the political left to Chuck Colson on the right, signed a "civility covenant ... calling for an end to the fight club tone of the national political discourse."[5] I doubt this covenant will deter the extremists, but it is a sign that the center-right Christians are alarmed enough by the threats of violence and vitriolic spew to say something about it. That's a good start.

We should celebrate the good news that the far-right mixture of evangelicalism with racial and gender prejudice is losing its power to bring young people into the fold. As pastor Carol Howard Merritt argues:

> Waging a culture war against "radical feminism," ... to a new generation of women ... didn't seem radical at all. It just felt like equality. We had men like Mike Huckabee teaching that the man is the head of the household and that the wife ought to "graciously submit" to him, but in a time when wives were just as educated and brought home just as much money as their husbands, domestic subjugation seemed unthinkable.
>
> In addition, the religious intolerance that many Evangelicals preached no longer made sense in our changing neighborhoods. ... [It] not only disrespected men and women of other faiths, but it even questioned the beliefs of other Christians who were not as socially conservative.
>
> Finally, the conservative politics drove us away. There were some progressive Evangelicals, yet their voices were sidelined far too often. For the last couple of decades, a majority of the movement began to find great power as the Christian Right. Partnering with the Republican Party, they began to extol an idealized view of the family, rallying against abortion and homosexual rights. Often the fixation on these two issues came at the expense of feeding the hungry and sheltering the homeless. Many Christian Right leaders brushed aside caring for the earth and mocked global climate change. Health care became demonized and wars glorified. So many Christian teachings became sacrificed for the Republican agenda that we hardly recognized our faith any longer. And so we left our congregations.[6]

We should also be heartened to see that a few people connected to the evangelical tradition are speaking out against the ways in which a collectivity of extremist narratives—in politics, in churches, in fiction, and in films—created a cultural surround that empowers the fringe hate groups and militias, and inspires them to violence. Consider the case of Frank Schaeffer, son of well-known evangelical leaders and author of two best-selling books, *Crazy for God* and *Patience With God*, documenting the problem. In his view, the "*Left Behind* cult" (sixteen books and over seventy million copies sold) and teleministries such as the one founded by Jack Impe have created an "End Times" paranoia that includes "people stocking up on assault rifles and ammunition, adopting 'Christ-centered' home school curricula, fearing higher education, embracing rumor as fact, and learning to love hatred for the 'other,' as exemplified by a revived anti-immigrant racism, the murder of doctors who do abortions, and even a killing in the Holocaust Museum."[7]

From this evangelical cultural surround supporting the Rush Limbaugh, Glenn Beck, Michael Savage, and Fox News et al. comes a totalizing narrative about progressives, that divides our nation into a politico-religious Us versus Them. Teabaggers joined the narrative, and exacerbated it. Sarah Palin and Michele Bachmann, John Boehner and Mitch McConnell, and others preach to the extremist choir, which, at the same time, further reduces any chance for finding common ground. Schaeffer concludes:

> The *Left Behind* franchise holds out hope for the self-disenfranchised that at last everyone will know "we" were right and "they" were wrong. They'll know because Spaceship Jesus will come back and whisk us away, leaving everyone else to ponder just how very lost they are because they refused to say the words, "I accept Jesus as my personal savior" and join our side while there was still time! Even better: Jesus will kill all those smart-ass, Democrat-voting, overeducated people who have been mocking us!

Until we all learn to speak out against this violent and divisive paranoia, until we literally crowd out the spread of hate from the social networks and mediated space that seems consumed by capitalizing on it and financially benefiting from it, the more hatred and division will dominate those channels and those networks. The more the overheated spectacle dominates the newscape and blogosphere and Facebook, the more visual and visceral encouragement is given to the enemy. It eggs on the bad behavior of an already maddening crowd.

And that maddening crowd is getting bolder. On April 2, 2010, it was widely reported that the FBI and the Department of Homeland Security were investigating an extremist group calling itself "The Guardians of the Free Republics," who had released thirty letters to governors of states asking them to resign within three days or face dire consequences.[8] Their mission, according to the group's website, is to "restore America" by peacefully dismantling parts of the government, although "peacefully" apparently includes threats, intimidation, and if that fails, forcing them from office. Somehow.

In some important ways, history is on our side. Mike Signer, in a blog called "How to Beat the Demagogues," compares much of the far-right rhetoric these days to what occurred after the passage of Social Security. The lessons for our leaders from that era include:

1. Ad hominem attacks can backfire.
2. Help educate people about our constitutional traditions.
3. Extreme opportunists usually self-destruct.
4. Side with the people and show them results.[9]

Signer concludes: "As we digest the recent turmoil, our leaders will need—just as in the 1930s—to educate, work with, and trust the body of the people. Figures like President Obama can emerge stronger than before, leaving melodramatic opportunists like Sarah Palin and Glenn Beck where they belong: in the wake of history."

Some minds won't change. Some people never learn. Some far right extremists are hell bent on making out of our political freedom a nightmarish civil war. In the previous chapters I've named some of them: Vanderbeogh, Beck, Palin, Limbaugh, Cheney, Coulter, a variety of armed militia groups such at the Hutaree, and so on. We cannot expect them to listen to us with open minds because they won't do it. They don't trust experts, or academics, any more than they trust Obama. And they share a common mindset that has crept into the mainstream. As Tom Halsted, writing in the *Huffington Post*, says: "A majority of Americans now do not believe in evolution, are convinced that global warming is a hoax, and are deeply suspicious of science and scientists, and all the other people they denounce as 'elitists.' It's scary. I hope it doesn't lead to widespread violence or political assassinations, but could easily imagine both happening."[10]

Given this irrational and hostile surround it may sound like a good idea to silence them through censorship laws or sanctions against their right to speak. But that is a short-term solution that will fail. As the ACLU has long argued, the cure for hate speech is more speech, not less speech. It pays to know what your enemy is thinking and saying. When they break laws, enforce the laws. Ours is a rule of law society.

But what we can and must do is unite around the cause of making America safe again for the muscular liberal narrative, for a counter-narrative capable of inspiring trust and confidence among ourselves and convincing to those who may yet be persuaded to our cause. We must unite to work for a society reconstituted around progressive values, *including those values that support a loyal opposition committed to the common good*. As I have repeated throughout this book and as President Obama has consistently underscored, it's the extremists who are our enemy, not all conservatives, and not all Republicans. We need political debate to maintain both our democracy and our status in the world.

We have a near enemy and a far enemy, and in some clear ways both enemies use similar communication tactics. Here is another lesson I have learned from monitoring the fear-inspired communication of Taliban leaders in Afghanistan that transfers rather directly to the American right wing's call for jihad. In Afghanistan, prior to democratic elections, Taliban leaders organize bands of terrorists to nail "Night Letters" to the doors of homes inhabited by potential voters.[11] The letters are explicit. They state that if members of this family vote, they will be killed. And not only the immediate voters, but all members of their families. So when I heard John Boehner call for Armageddon and explain that a colleague who changed his vote was a "dead man," I heard in those expressions an American mediated version of the Taliban Night Letter. Boehner's speech is the speech of a petty tyrant, a terrorist, not a statesman.

Caroline Myss sums up the domestic threat nicely:

Here's the bottom line, folks: The Republican right-wingers are dangerous. They should be considered homeland and homegrown security threats and we—those of us who live and vote on the other side of the aisle—are their targets. How do I know if one of these gun-toting hysterics won't let loose and "shoot to kill," following the orders of their leader, Sarah Palin? And, if Palin's too busy because of her upcoming Reality television series, I can easily imagine Michele Bachmann or John Boehner giving a "shoot to kill" command to their Tea Party followers.[12]

Myss's words were underscored on March 29, 2010, when the FBI raided the militia camp organized under the name the Hutaree and arrested nine men, who they charged with sedition:

> They were part of a group of apocalyptic Christian militants who were plotting to kill law enforcement officers in hopes of inciting an antigovernment uprising, the latest in a recent surge in right-wing militia activity.
>
> The court filing said the group, which called itself the Hutaree, planned to kill an unidentified law enforcement officer and then bomb the funeral caravan using improvised explosive devices based on designs used against American troops by insurgents in Iraq.[13]

This group had posted a YouTube video showing their training, their arms, and their intentions.[14] Once again I was reminded of the same recruitment-to-the-cause and fear tactics of our enemies overseas. But moreover I was struck by the Hutaree plan to use IEDs based on the ones used against our forces in Iraq and Afghanistan. That our homegrown extremists learn their ways from the extremists over there ought to sound a clear warning about how these militia think about the future. The good news is that this time the FBI stepped in before the group carried out its threats.

We have a near enemy and a far enemy. And they now share not only a narrative about the world but also weapons strategies. That cannot be allowed to continue unaddressed by our leaders or our law enforcement agencies. But it also requires something from each of us. We have been silent too long. We have allowed the far right to work its way into the mainstream, or at least so close to the mainstream as to be a free-flowing tributary of it. We have mostly ignored them. We have hoped they would simply fade away. They will not fade away.

Third, we must learn from our enemies, but with a rhetorical twist: we can no longer ignore toxic messages from extremists. Our neglect of the threat extremists pose, our lack of a coordinated counter-narrative response to the verbal IEDs of right wing talk show hosts, celebrity politicians, and pundits has only enabled their toxic message to permeate the media, to top best-seller lists, and to gain support over time in the same tried and true way that all propaganda gains support over time—by repeating the same lies, the same innuendos, and the same slogans until they begin to sound like the truth because we have heard them so long.

And, unfortunately, it is working to our enemy's advantage. According to a Pew Research poll in April 2010, about *80 percent of Americans said they did not trust our government.*[15] As my colleague, the Islamic scholar Jeff Halverson, put it:

> If 80% of AMERICANS don't trust the US govt, how could we ever expect Muslims overseas to trust it? The anti-govt sentiment at home isn't exactly a shining beacon for spreading democracy to the far regions of the earth either. If folks in the US are up in arms over the idea of healthcare reform, gay marriage rights, and (insert grievance here), how do we speak to Muslims in Iraq who lack electricity and basic sanitation in Sadr City? Or Afghanis in Kandahar? If we can't sell the U. S. govt to people in suburban America, with all its material delights, how do we sell it to a Palestinian family subsisting in Gaza? Funny how Americans can be so critical of domestic policy, and then so defensive and insular about foreign policy.[16]

One sad tenet of communication theory that progressives cannot afford to ignore: *once a message is "out there," you cannot take it back.* As a result, right wing reports of the findings of this Pew Research Center study and its toxic echo will remain part of our national consciousness for a long, long time. It may hamper the Obama administration's ability to gain public approval or support for reform legislation, particularly if those bills suggest that we are altering the balance of power from states to the federal government. It will continue to embolden Tea Party types and energize conservatives. It may hamper our foreign policy. At the very least, this study and its conclusions will be repeated in conversations and passed on through social networks and the news industry, find its way into comedy routines, and get quoted in books, such as this one. Here's another communication truth: once a message is "out there," those listeners who pass it along will be far less likely to question it, no matter how strong the opposing arguments may be, no matter what the truth is.

So, once again, my progressive friend, what should we do? So far in this little volume I've outlined problems and opportunities that our speech, our teaching, and our writing must address. But I have not yet explained how to build a new progressive core narrative. To do that requires learning some additional narrative lessons from our president, and from our enemies.

George Lakoff believes that one of the chief advantages used by radical conservatives is the power of linguistic framing in an efficient and effective communication system that operates 24/7.[17] For example, at least since Reagan, radical conservatives have been largely successful in branding taxes as an evil force in America, despite the fact that we need them to "provide for the common welfare and promote the common defense." So much so, Lakoff argues, that over the years their repeated attacks on the idea of taxes as something akin to a greedy politician taking money out of our wallet has created a brain change for most people: when we hear the word "taxes" it triggers "*my* taxes" instead.

To counter this framing of taxes as evil, Democrats have often adopted the same language in the hope that by using it, they will gain support from those in the middle or on the right who might otherwise go the other way. We, too, are against unnecessary taxes. But borrowing this conservative framing device has had an unintended side effect. Lakoff concludes: "The use of the language of the right can move them [Democrats] to think like conservatives, and hence to vote like conservatives." In the end, we have convinced ourselves only that taxes are bad so we are reluctant if not downright opposed to making the raising of any taxes part of our core narrative. But taking a longer view, and examining the projections of the Congressional Budget Office, there is no denying the facts: unless we find some way to generate money, all discretionary spending will cease by 2020. We will have on hand only enough money to pay the interest on our burgeoning debt and the Pentagon's budget. So what must be done?

A more productive communication strategy is to reframe taxes as something listeners and readers associate with positive outcomes. Instead of calling them "taxes," which sounds burdensome and provokes even among those sympathetic to our cause an instantaneous Pavlovian response, let's refer to them as "revenue." *Revenue* provides us with roads, schools, police, firefighters, community gyms, protection from our enemies, and a host of other necessary things. It is one important way we contribute to the common good. President Obama, on "tax day," April 15, 2010, embraced this new way of talking about revenues while at the same time chastising the Tea Party. In fact, under his administration 95 percent of Americans pay less tax than we ever have, and a full 47 percent of us paid no taxes at all in 2010. By reframing taxes as something Democrats reduced while at the same time embracing the idea of new revenues to promote the general welfare and provide for the common defense, Obama also *reframed what had been a binary opposition into a new dialectical tension.* Just as he had done earlier in his Nobel Prize address, he complicated our thinking and significantly reduced the ability of the far right to gain a rhetorical upper hand.

Given the Pew Center study, however, it is pretty clear that the harder narrative work is reclaiming *the idea that government can do good things for people.* That government is competent. That it is capable of handling the new responsibilities that a progressive president believes it must and that a long view of our mission requires in order to succeed. This narrative task is doubly difficult because, as extensive psychological studies have demonstrated, "bad is stronger than good."[18] After an exhaustive survey of this idea across a wide range of human activities and relationships, the conclusion for us to consider in light of the Pew Center findings is this one: "Bad impressions and

bad stereotypes are quicker to form and more resistant to disconfir-
mation than good ones." So again, what should we do?

Put simply, we know we cannot allow negative stereotypes of our
government to prevail or else we risk losing The Battle of Narratives.
Good government is the cornerstone of our progressive agenda. A
good government made up of decent, hard working people who
believe in public service and who want to do what is right—that is the
message we must carry into our classrooms, our campuses, and our
communities, and support for that message must be in the human
stories that we should be celebrating.

Furthermore, we must tell personal stories that reveal not
only why we need the government to protect our rights and level
the playing field of opportunity, but personal stories that embody
success—in the form of prosperity, justice, community, and happi-
ness—when good government works for all of us. I began this book
with one shining example of President Obama's use of a personal
story about a child in Virginia willing to open his piggybank to help
his father pay a medical bill to underscore the power of stories to
motivate understanding and empathy. But once again, we cannot
solely rely on our president to be the only one telling those stories.
We must encourage others to the progressive vision via our own personal examples, our own stories. We have been silent in the face of
brutish right-wing rhetoric celebrating the triumph of the individual
at all costs to the detriment of our collective well being. We must tell
a different story to America for America to change.

I hate to admit it, but the far right is better in the deployment of
personal narratives than we are. Watch Glenn Beck. Listen to Rush
Limbaugh. Read Sarah Palin's blog. They are chock full of examples
drawn from their (often mythic) childhoods, from stories they have
been told by "real people," and with emotional accounts of persons
and places that reveal the tellers of these tales to be just like everyone
else in "mainstream America." They glorify the individual in an age of
self-absorption. From a rhetorical vantage, it is a classic case of identification of the speaker with an audience, and it is one of the most
powerful tools for persuasion in any narrative toolbox.[19]

Another important tool is what communication theorist Ernest Bormann, in his classic study of religious and political revivals designed to "restore the American Dream," calls "fantasy themes."[20] These fantasy themes are rooted in a mythic past and are used to unify a shared vision of community. As I've shown, American extremists have a well-honed master narrative that serves as a fantasy theme about restoring the American Dream and that unifies a right wing audience with a mythic vision of America constructed according to their beliefs.

By contrast, progressives have not yet unified around a common rhetorical vision, and hence, we claim no commonplace of sound-bites, no storehouse of storylines, to support our core narrative. Ours is a collectivity of diverse political communities organized around core values—which is a good start—but that as yet have not been used to clearly articulate a common vision. One result of our narrative failure is that we have for too long allowed the far right to usurp the beautiful idea of America as a tolerant nation open to diverse people and ways of life in which government functions to "promote the general welfare and provide for the common defense." Another result has been the extreme right's hijacking of the American Dream, substituting a communal vision grounded in the pragmatic value of providing care and assistance for one's neighbors and one's community, an entirely corrupt individualist and hypercapitalist vision perhaps best exemplified by the Reagan-era bumpersticker "He Who Dies With the Most Toys Wins."

In the Battle of Narratives we have some narrative catching up to do.

Interestingly enough, a relatively obscure presidential candidate named Barack Obama gave a powerful speech on the idea of the American Dream on November 7, 2007, in Bettendorf, Iowa. In it he offered what I consider a clear statement of the communal unifying principle of our progressive version of the American Dream:

> What is unique about America is that we want these dreams for more than ourselves—we want them for each other. That's why we call it the American dream. We want it for the kid who doesn't go to college because she cannot afford it; for the worker who is wondering if his wages will pay this winter's heating bill; for 47

million Americans living without health care; for the millions more who worry if they have enough to retire with the dignity they have earned.

When our fellow Americans are denied the American dream, our own dreams are diminished. And today, the cost of that dream is rising faster than ever before. While some have prospered beyond imagination in this global economy, middle-class Americans—as well as those working hard to become middle class—are seeing the American dream slip further and further away....

There has been a lot of talk in this campaign about the politics of hope. But the politics of hope doesn't mean hoping that things come easy. It's a politics of believing in things unseen; of believing in what this country might be; and of standing up for that belief and fighting for it when it's hard.

America is the sum of our dreams. And what binds us together, what makes us one American family, is that we stand up and fight for each other's dreams, that we reaffirm that fundamental belief—I am my brother's keeper, I am my sister's keeper—through our politics, our policies, and in our daily lives. It's time to do that once more. It's time to reclaim the American dream.[21]

That so many of us wanted to believe in our collective ability to reclaim that American dream is one major reason why Barack Obama was elected president. That we now need to carry into our own communities his rhetorical vision of that progressive version of the American dream should be clear. But his statement, even when repeated and even if translated into a popular soundbite and/or bumpersticker, only represents one part of the necessary storyline. For our belief in the American Dream (capitals intended) may only be realized if *we also provide* compelling storylines that align our values, our policy objectives, and our personal examples with that vision.

To review: if we can accomplish these basic communication goals we will have the beginnings of a counter-narrative advantage:

- Speak out against toxic messages and messengers;
- Honor those on the right and those in evangelical communities who share the long view;

- Reframe key words and phrases;
- Use the power of our personal stories to give a human face to good government; and
- Craft an easily reproduced rhetorical vision out of the conjoined stuff of Obama's American Dream and our own.
- Speak out when the media gets it wrong or only focuses on those groups that threaten to take us backward rather than forward.

These everyday rhetorical moves must involve all of us acting together for the greater good. The urgency of our mission is why we cannot wait any longer to act. That is why we must get out in front of our president; our representatives; our leaders in local communities; our churches and synagogues and mosques and meeting rooms; among our colleagues and in our classrooms; and communicate for the common good. We on the left cannot any longer afford to be labeled as weak; we cannot tolerate being tarred with the "L-word" brush as if it were a curse and just "let it slide"; and we cannot be silent when the far right's toxic messages are deployed.

Our counter-narrative must be an everyday communication activity. Together, we must be muscular and our voices must be strong. We must be compelling as well as inspiring, and capable of reclaiming the disputed terrain called the American Dream. We must use our voices and our communication to win the hearts and minds of our country. We must appeal not only to those who agree with us, but also to those who civilly disagree with us—Republicans, Independents, and Conservatives. Regardless of our differences, we all need to stand up and move against the violent extremists on the far right.

This counter-narrative must become our new passion. Our source of common strength.

Stand up! We are America's Patriots! Volunteer for this vital duty!

Let our counter-narrative campaign begin…

Academics, this is a call to arms! If you are an historian, call your local news outlet or send an email to Fox and CNN and explain why the Tea Party claims are not historically accurate. Call them on their misuse of history. If you are an economist, run the numbers yourself and then send the results to the newspaper to show why the right's economic claims about the relationship of taxes to deficits are not only inaccurate but dangerous. If you are a communication scholar, give interviews explaining how the rhetoric used by hate groups works and what people should be aware of when they hear these types of messages. All of us—psychology professors, biologists, religious studies scholars—all of us working in and for the academy owe it to ourselves and to our communities to come down from the ivory tower and engage our enemies in the public sphere.

They fear us, partially because they don't know us. Those who vilify "the intellectual elite" might be surprised to find that we worry about money, take our kids to school and ball practice, run errands, and live pretty much as they do. Their misconception of who we are and what we do is partially our fault. It is a result of convincing ourselves that what we have to offer is not for public consumption and/ or that it is up to others to carry on this fight against stupidity, injustice, and greed.

Here's the bottom-line: if what we do every day is not something to further the goals of a progressive society, if the fruits of our labor are not used to solve our problems and bring us together as a force for good for our people and as a nation, then ultimately our enemies are right: intellectuals are a waste of time and money. We will lose this Battle of Narratives, and with it, the beautiful idea of America.

7. The Core Counter-Narrative

This book would be incomplete without offering a core counter-narrative. Originally I had not intended to draft one, but my wife—an excellent editor and collaborator—reached the end of the previous chapter, and in a fit of exasperation, told me flat out that I was letting readers down without one. "But who am I to suggest America's story?" I complained. "I'm not the president. I'm not an elected leader. I'm just an ordinary guy, a khaki-pants-and-blue-shirt-wearing teacher and scholar with some progressive ideas."

"Exactly," she replied. "You are one of us. You are exactly like the people you are urging into the fight. And, after all, you are encouraging them to add their voice to this 'Battle of Narratives.' You owe it to them to add yours."

I hate it when she uses my own stance against me. So here it is. I'm not going to apologize for it—I teach students never to apologize in advance of a speech. I offer this as a starting point from which to build a *cohesive* progressive narrative.

Until quite recently, the story of the United States of America is a story of the triumph of hope over fear, of our success as a nation in promoting peace and prosperity against tyranny and want, of establishing equal justice under the law for all, and of creating—out of nothing more or less powerful than words on a piece of parchment—a set of defining principles and rights that have inspired us and guided us as a nation for well over 200 years.

Our Founding Fathers built into both the Declaration of Independence and the Constitution of the United States that *government* is the guiding light of justice, freedom, and democracy. It was in *government*, not kings, that our Founding Fathers placed their trust. Where did government reside for the Founding Fathers? Now as it did in 1776, it resides in the people specifically, in those who "deriving their just powers from the consent of the governed" and through the process of election, in those who elect them. The Founding Fathers, in their infinite wisdom, cautioned against those who would attempt to change "governments long established . . . for light and transient causes." While kings and "despots" could be overthrown, governments "by and for the people" in the words of the Founding Fathers had to be handled with prudence.

Prudence is an old fashioned word. It means caution, carefulness, and good sense. It means that conclusions are drawn with forethought and through the power of reasoning. The opposite of prudence is recklessness. In using the word *prudence* the Founding Fathers warned us not to be reckless where government was concerned. Only after a "long train of abuses and usurpations" did the Founding Fathers even begin to consider revolution. Indeed, the Revolutionary War, fueled by a string of usurpations large and small by the King and his representatives in the colonies, took place over decades. It was not simply caused by the taxation of tea, as the Tea Party would have us believe; revolutions are rarely that simple or superficial. For the Founding Fathers, overthrowing a king and replacing him with a government "by and for the people" came after years of petitioning the King to treat the colonies fairly and allow them equal representation in Parliament.

Ironically, the next section of the Declaration of Independence is perhaps the most telling, but it is also the most commonly overlooked, particularly by those on the right who like to cherry-pick their use of the Founding Fathers' words. Crucial to the success of the colonies was the ability of the colonists to enact *laws*. Their first attack against the King was that he refused "Assent to Laws, the most wholesome and necessary for the public good." Laws for the *public good*. Laws not to uphold the rights of a single individual, but for the *public good*. Not laws to govern the rights of corporations or for the rights of corporations masquerading as individuals, but for the *public good*. While a string of other issues follow, each important and crucial for the development of a strong government, the refusal of the King to "Assent to Laws . . . for the public good" was the number one concern of the Founding Fathers.

Why is this history lesson important? Because the radical right and its ill-informed followers *use* the Founding Fathers and our founding documents to further a dangerous and ill-conceived anti-democratic, anti-American, and anti-government agenda. They take one line from the Declaration giving the people the right "to alter or abolish" destructive government, without heeding the many prudent cautions the Founding Fathers used when they made this statement. They would rather destroy our democratic way of life than to abide by the "consent of the people." Rather than risk losing power, they would rather put our entire democracy at risk, by calling into question the right of a duly elected government to govern. They would, as Sarah Palin, Michael Savage, Michele Bachmann, and Glenn Beck have done a number of times, call individuals to arms to uphold individuals rights, rather than pull together for the *public good* that was at the forefront of the Founding Fathers' need for governmental change.

For the Founding Fathers, the debate over the principled change and modification of our laws is the true business of government, and that government—in order to be worthy of respect—must be responsive to the *changing needs* of its citizens. That is why the Constitution lays out three branches of government, and that is why there are checks and balances placed on each branch. That is why we hold regular elections and that is why the concept of "new" legislation, while often painful, seems as natural to us as the birth of a child.

As we have grown as a nation, so has our need for government. When we were only thirteen newly formed states, we required only the Constitution and ten Amendments. But over time, as the nation grew and as our thoughts and ideas about democracy changed we added amendments to reflect these changes. This ability to remain true to our values and to our beliefs, but to be profoundly open to change, profoundly open to improving our lives and the lives of our fellow citizens, and profoundly open to seeking a common good that enables all of us to achieve the American Dream is what makes America great.

However, there are those who don't share this passion for progress and who do not support change. Historically, those citizens have represented diverse interests and ambitions, but at the core of their opposition to change has always been the same unwavering belief in their own privilege, in the belief that their rights as individuals are more important than upholding the *public good*. This land was *their* land, not our land. It didn't matter if their issue was property rights, slavery, voting rights, women's rights, war, trade, or taxation, they have always held that less government is the best government. Because less government means that life remains the same. The old rules—the ones that vest power in the privileged few—always apply. That no one "interferes" with "their" business. That no one "redistributes the wealth." That "freedom" means "free," by God!

And that is the fundamental difference. It is at the heart of the political catchphrases of unrestrained capitalism that have become convenient mediated soundbites—soundbites that, when they are so often repeated, have become toxic to the American way of life. The core of the "us versus them" argument that clearly spells out the difference between the left and the right is that those of us on the left believe in the trust, justice, and power the Founding Fathers placed in *government*, and that it is the job of the government, elected individuals, and people employed by government to first and foremost provide for the *public good*. By contrast, the right believes that the rights of the individual trump those of the American people.

Contrary to what those who oppose change want you to believe, progressives are not anti-capitalists. Nor do we want to interfere with your business. Nor redistribute the wealth. Nor deny the power of freedom. It's just that we view those elements of the American way of life differently. We have learned what happens when our desire not to interfere with your business led to unfair or unethical practices. When our willingness to go along with your "trickle" down theory of economics did not, in fact, trickle down but instead created an unprecedented redistribution of wealth from the middle classes to the upper classes.

That created the metaphorical "bubble" in markets that could not be sustained and that led to home foreclosures and bankruptcies and high rates of unemployment for millions of our fellow citizens. And we have cried—literally cried—over the end result of unregulated, untaxed "freedom" in the Gulf of Mexico, and in the City of New Orleans, and in many other cities and towns that today find themselves cleaning up ecological, material, and infrastructure disasters that could have been avoided or at the very least mitigated through stronger regulation administered by vigilant government organizations.

We have learned that freedom is best when it is coupled *with* public responsibility. We have seen first-hand how easy it is for elected officials on the right to decry big government until they need government to step in and make things right as Bobby Jindal and Haley Barbour did after the BP oil disaster in the Gulf of Mexico. And as did Republican governors when they found their states' budget crises insurmountable without federal help.

We have seen first hand, if we have a strong government in place, lead by qualified people, we can weather any storm. In the 1990s, President Clinton appointed James Lee Witt to head the Federal Emergency Management Agency—FEMA. He was the first FEMA director with actual emergency-management experience. By 1996, FEMA and Witt were receiving praise for providing "sterling disaster relief." George Bush replaced Witt, who by all accounts was doing an exemplary job, with Joe Allbaugh. Allbaugh sent Michael Brown to oversee FEMA's response to Katrina, and we all know how that turned out. You did a heck of a job, Brownie! The point is neither Allbaugh or Brown had any experience in emergency management. Both were political appointees. Both represent what happens when we think of government as merely political and not an extension of the public good.

When people—at least some of those we elect and the rest of us who care about this country—take seriously their charge to uphold the *public good*, when we have had a strong government in place, working *alongside* of enterprise, working as *partners* to continued growth, prosperity, education, health care, energy, and justice, government no longer becomes the last resort when things go horribly wrong, but instead is *the engine that fuels our progress.*

For this engine to function smoothly and efficiently, however, requires a change in our narrative about the role of government in a democratic society. Changing the narrative requires two things. Neither of them is easy; both are worthwhile.

First, we need to reverse thirty years of propaganda from those who oppose change designed to convince Americans that government is bad, that taxes are bad, and that regulation is bad. We need to defeat those extremist messages not because we simply disagree philosophically with them, but because they have proven to be wrong time and time again. Look around. The evidence of their wrongness— their "focused wrongness"— is everywhere apparent. Those who continue to support that focused wrongness will not back down, nor ever admit they have been wrong. They are focused. And they think they are right. So they must be defeated in the polls, in the schools, in the media, in our classrooms, and at the voting booth.

The second thing we need to do is learn to think of government— and talk about government—in human terms. Government isn't a monolith. It is made up of women and men of all ages, colors, religions, and backgrounds who get up early every day and go to work. Most days they come home late. They are not faceless bureaucrats. They are your neighbors. They are your friends. Your colleagues. Your brothers and sisters. Your parents and your children. Government is the men and women serving in the Armed Forces; they are the people who inspect our meat and keep our food safe; they are the people who ensure that Social Security checks, Medicare, and Medicaid payments are made. They are the doctors and nurses who tend to our veterans, our children, and our elderly. And yes they are the members of the House, the Senate, and the Obama administration. These people work for America, which means they work for you and for me. Most of them are hard working, intelligent, and capable human beings who each and every day ensure that we don't have another terrorist attack, who ensure that our streets are safe, our laws are upheld, and that our freedoms are protected. At the state level, they are the people who fight the fires, teach students, repair roads, and serve in the National Guard. Government is not an evil institution in our life. It is made up of good people who make our lives *better.* Who provide for the *public good.*

For too long, we have allowed those who refuse to work for the common good, and those from the far right who run for elected office on campaigns of fear, to define government—not as the Founding Fathers intended, not as an instrument of justice, freedom, and democracy for all—but as a faceless entity to fear and hate. Some use this fear and hate to call for a return to a mythic past, to a time when rich white males ruled the land at the expense of everyone else. Those on the far right who espouse this "return" narrative honestly don't believe in equal rights, or in fairness, or in justice. Nor do they believe that schools should be supported, or that health care should be available to everyone. Who wants an educated electorate? Educated people embrace progress and change, ask critical questions, and are not satisfied with the way things are. Educated people are dangerous. Educated people are in favor of programs such as affordable health care, whereas "right-minded" people see "health care reform" as a cause, perpetrated by liberals, that benefits only the poor, the unemployed, and the illegal immigrants who run up our health care costs and, if truth be told, who don't deserve our mercy or our care. Left to their own devices, these "return" narrativist, these far-right spokespersons and the enemies of progress would put our economy in permanent peril in order to preserve their precious tax cuts, despite what the best economic minds in the country—indeed, in the world—say about that. They would also put the world's environment in permanent unregulated peril to underscore their false beliefs about global warming, despite all the good science to the contrary.

Is this the America you want? I don't think it is. So what must be done?

The first step is the step we take together. I am asking for all of us to join in a concerted counter-narrative campaign to overturn thirty years of propaganda that has come very close to destroying the beautiful idea that is America. We must collectively imagine a better future, a more progressive future, a bolder future, before we can enter it, and that act of imagination must come complete with a commitment to convince others of the rightness and of the radiance of our vision. Ours is a way forward that is open to everyone. Our aim is to provide for the common defense and promote the general welfare, again, for everyone. We can only accomplish that by understanding that our government is a good thing, that the people who work for us do have our best interests at heart, and that new creative partnerships between government and the private sector will be made that benefit us all.

Finally, we need to always remember that America is a work in progress, with the emphasis on progress. We are not finished making it yet. We still have a long way to go. But with your help, with all of us working together, we can do the good work that must be done. We can believe, once again, in the American Dream.

From the core narrative I have proposed emerge a variety of specific issues, all of which can be made stronger because they share the same narrative muscle. For me, there are everyday issues, and then there are core issues. Once again, I consider the core issues as integral to a longer view of our narrative campaign. Below are my suggestions.

1. The purpose of government, according to our Constitution, is simple: "to provide for the common defense, and to promote the general welfare." Government has real work to do, and our founders were wise in recognizing that these two tasks require a strong central organization to carry them out. As a result, our government provides for the common defense and we have the strongest military in the world. We have yet to attain "the general welfare" equivalent to other modern nations. But we can. Health care reform is part of it, and although it is not a perfect solution, it is a progressive step in the right direction. Let's continue to improve on it. Let's continue to hold our leaders responsible for its proper management.

2. The key to promoting the general welfare is electing better representatives of progressive ideas to Congress. That means electing people who are smarter, better prepared for leadership, and better able to foster the creative partnerships between government and the private sector we need, not the same tired old puppets of special interests or lobbyists on either side of the aisle

who make staying in office their true occupation. The key to fair elections is campaign finance reform. It's that simple. McCain-Feingold was a step in the right direction, but most politicians did not take advantage of it because they didn't have to. As a result, our politicians are in office because *money buys elections.* And to get the money to buy the election, and to remain in office, requires a constant campaign of appearances and fund-raisers. Until that changes, our elected representatives will continue to disappoint us. They will continue to be in the pockets of large corporations and private donors. And good people who would otherwise consider running for public office will shy away. I say this is what we should do:

a. Introduce legislation that limits campaign spending to the amount of the salary the person elected would earn doing the job for two years. Provide the money for all campaigns through the proceeds of a national lottery and voluntary contributions up to ten dollars per person on the annual IRS form.

b. Limit the term of all elected officials to six years. If the State Department limits the tour of duty for foreign service officers to three years because of the likelihood of undue influence being exerted on them, this same logic should be applied to members of Congress and the Presidency. At the same time, continue the Obama initiative to significantly regulate membership and further demand reform from the professional lobbying community.

c. Create a special fund (again, from the national lottery) to promote Constitutional and Congressional literacy for the general public. Offer courses at community colleges, develop a resource website, sponsor online and televised programs designed to provide citizens with information about current and proposed bills before Congress and the testimony of experts on subjects under consideration.

d. Demand transparency in all things election: it is in the public interest to seek out information on corporations and private donors responsible for financing each and every significant public elected official; require that this information be publicized.

3. Speak out against extremists, near and far. Do not ignore them. Ask elected representatives to speak out against them. Require accountability if they fail to do so. Make their stance on extremist issues a matter of public record. If they refuse to address these issues, ask why. If they still refuse to answer, organize and campaign against them. They do not have the best interests of the United States of America in their hearts or minds.

4. Work for legislation to end foreign ownership of our news media. Mediated communication is the most powerful national resource we have for promoting and defending ideas and policies. We cannot afford the luxury of media being manipulated by non-U.S. citizens solely for profit at the expense of the truth. If we stop foreign countries from owning our ports on the grounds that they could use such access to import dangerous materials, then we should use the same reasoning to argue against foreigners having direct access to the media on the grounds that they can use that access to deploy dangerous ideas and spark even more dangerous and divisive controversies.

5. Stop watching Fox News. If viewers turn away, so too will sponsors. If sponsors turn away, the show won't last. When you enter a public place and see that Fox News is on the television, ask to change it. My wife does this at the bank, in restaurants, and at the gym. She simply says, "Would you mind changing the channel to something else?" More often than not, the channel is changed without a thought. Occasionally, someone will ask why and she replies, "Because as a customer, I don't feel I should be exposed to political views I find offensive. I'll be happy to take my business elsewhere if changing the channel is a problem." She has never had to ask twice.

6. Work to elect Democrats who uphold Democratic principles and work to replace those who do not. The Ben Nelsons, the Joe

Liebermans and the Blanche Lincolns who claim Democratic Party status and sponsorship need to work for us, not for their own interests or the special interests that line their pockets. When they say boneheaded things, our outrage should be widespread and immediate. When they do boneheaded things, we must demand their recall. And we must ensure—by our promise to withdraw financial support—that our leaders in the House and the Senate hold members accountable to us, the voters. We can no longer tolerate their collective dysfunction or their hypocrisy. We cannot simply shrug our collective shoulders and go on with our lives, which they, in conjunction with a 24-hour news cycle and our increasingly short attention span, have learned to count on.

7. Support progressives nationally who are fighting the good fight. Representative Anthony Weiner from New York and Representative Alan Grayson from Florida are two of the toughest members of the House we have, and they deserve our support. When you see an elected official standing up and doing the right thing, send an email and thank them, or, better yet, send a small donation and free up more of their time to actually govern.

These ideas are only a beginning. But they represent steps I believe we must take in forwarding a progressive narrative that can change our world for the better. None of the ideas is especially new, and I don't claim to have come up with them on my own. I believe they are core arguments that have been underrepresented in the public marketplace of ideas and that they must be articulated anew by all of us who claim the pragmatic progressive label.

For each of the points listed above, please develop your own local examples. Your own personal narratives. Fact-check them. Connect them to the American Dream.

You might be wondering why I haven't included a host of other critical social justice issues in the core counter-narrative. For example, what about immigration policy? What about global warming? What about a woman's right to choose? Gay access to marriage? And so on. Those are *issues*. To be successful, we need to understand the difference between issues and a *core narrative*. Immigration reform fits within the larger narrative of what is in the best public interest. The issue is how it is accomplished. An issue is what fits within the core narrative, rather than what defines it. Issues should enhance the narrative, not undermine it or divide it or tear it apart. So when issues come up, we should be quick to say things like "of course Democrats support immigration reform. It is within the best interests of all Americans to have strong borders and strong immigration reform policies." Don't get tangled up or sidetracked by the issues when we are talking core narrative.

While these issues and others are important and deserve our attention and action, it is far more important to *first get our core counter-narrative across to the general public*. Until we accomplish that goal, we lack a common identity capable of combating extremists' attacks on us and on the America we want to live in, raise children in, invest in, and love. When we lack a core narrative about what good government can do, the gap between us and the American people drives every other critical issue that requires it. Until we are successful in reestablishing the value and power of good government within an overarching narrative of a communal American Dream, we cannot hope to accomplish social justice for everyone, much less achieve credible national policies about immigration or exert international leadership on global warming. By dividing ourselves into competing issue camps vested only in our own pet concerns, we will accomplish only our own defeat.

One final lesson from the counter-terrorism literature must be underscored: combating extremism is a form of communication, just as extremism itself is.[1] Extremists receive and interpret progressive narratives about what we value—what we consider acceptable and decent what we consider wrong. Extremists seek to distort our messages by turning them into catchy soundbites, pejorative labels, and plain folksy metaphors in order to support their core ideological narrative and its profound sense of fear, loathing, intolerance, and injustice. Everything we progressives advocate becomes a sign of their apocalypse. Their anger becomes their way of legitimating their warrant. The street becomes their theatre, the entertainment news their friend. They play it up loud for public audiences and use social networks and the Internet to spread their ideology.

We are, like America after 9/11, playing a cultural game of catch-up. Our enemies have a core narrative. They have media attention and coverage. They know what they are doing. We haven't taken what they are doing or them seriously enough. We can't seem to comprehend how it is that a loosely organized band of older grumpy white people who blame the government for everything and who don't want to pay taxes successfully hijacked the political landscape while our man Barack Obama was president.

It is time to act.

Those of us in academic life have been more or less content to stay home and attend to other things in the hope that someone out there would do something about it. In this way, we progressive academics resemble our country in the lead-up to 9/11. We ignored the signs. As a result, we have been careless about surveillance and negligent if not dismissive of attacks threatened against us. The image of the liberal, of the progressive, has been the subject of humor and ridicule in the public sphere. More worried about our own mortgages, our jobs, our families, our own institutions, and our comfortable lives than about the steady erosion of our national narrative, we have simply persevered. Unwilling to do the hard emotional labor of connecting the dots for ourselves and for others, we Doctors of Philosophy and others of similar ilk have been largely irrelevant to the ongoing war of ideas.

But that time is over. It *must be* over.

Together, we can restore the American Dream of the Founding Fathers to its rightful owners, the American people—rich, poor and middle class. We can foster a new beginning where government is part of the solution, where prudence is once again respected and understood, and where the common good triumphs over self-interest.

Notes

Preface

1. Eric Boehlert, "Post-Hutaree: How Glenn Beck and Fox News Spread The Militia Message," *Huffington Post*, April 6, 2010. http://www.huffingtonpost.com/eric-boehlert/post-hutaree-how-glenn-be_b_526687.html

2. Timothy Egan, "The Desert Derangement Syndrome," *New York Times*, April 28, 2010. http://opinionator.blogs.nytimes.com/2010/04/28/desert-derangement-syndrome/?ref=opinion

3. For overview of the new conservative dilemma, see Patricia Cohen, "'Epistemic Closure'? Those Are Fighting Words," *New York Times Book Review*, April 27, 2010. http://www.nytimes.com/2010/04/28/books/28conserv.html?ref=books

4. Ibid.

5. For those unfamiliar with this text, a quick overview may be found at http://en.wikipedia.org/wiki/Ideas_Have_Consequences

6. George Nash, "Reappraising the Right: The Past and Future of American Conservatism." Lecture may be accessed at http://www.heritage.org/Research/Lecture/Reappraising-the-Right-The-Past-and-Future-of-American-Conservatism

7. Patricia Cohen, "'Epistemic Closure'? Those Are Fighting Words." *New York Times Book Review*, April 27, 2010. http://www.nytimes.com/2010/04/28/books/28conserv.html?ref=books.

8. Danny Shea, "Cable News Rating April 2010," *The Huffington Post*, April 27, 2010. http://www.huffingtonpost.com/2010/04/28/cable-news-ratings-april_n_554295.html

Introduction: Before We Begin

1.   George Lakoff, *Don't Think of an Elephant: Know Your Values and Frame the Debate*. (White River Junction, VT: Chelsea Green Publishing Company, 2004), 94. Thanks to Sarah Jane Tracy for reminding me of this framing schema and directing me to reread the book.

2.   Howard Dean, "Foreword," in George Lakoff, *Don't Think of an Elephant: Know Your Values and Frame the Debate* (White River Junction, VT: Chelsea Green Publishing Company, 2004).

3.   George Lakoff, "The Obama Code," *Daily Kos*, February 24, 2009. http://www. dailykos.com/story/2009/2/24/04124/0642/643/701081

4.   See, for example, Robert L. Scott and Donald K. Smith, "The Rhetoric of Confrontation," *The Quarterly Journal of Speech*, 60, 1 (November 1969):1–8.

5.   Office of the Press Secretary, The White House. http://www.whitehouse.gov/ the_press_office/RemarksbyPresidentBarackObamaOnChildrensHealthInsuranceProgramBillSigning/

6.   Bernard Bailyn, *The Ideological Origins of the American Revolution* (Cambridge, MA: Belknap/Harvard University Press, 1992), 323.

Chapter 1. The Battle of Narratives

1.   This paragraph is intended to be read as a parody of and tribute to the opening paragraph in Karl Marx's *The Communist Manifesto*.

2.   W. R. Fisher, *Human communication as narration: Toward a philosophy of reason, value, and action* (Columbia: University of South Carolina Press, 1987).

3.   My use of this perjorative term is entirely intentional; please see why, as well as a partial apology for it, in chapter 2.

4.   Daniel Nasaw, "Sarah Palin's hand crib notes mocked by White House aide." http://www.guardian.co.uk/world/2010/feb/10/sarah-palin-hand-crib-notes -white-house

5.   John Avlon, "Scary New GOP Poll: Wingnuts Hijacking Politics." http://www.thedailybeast.com/blogs-and-stories/2010-03-22/ scary-new-gop-poll/?cid=hp:exc

6.   H. L. Goodall, Jr., *Writing Qualitative Inquiry: Self, Stories, and Academic Life* (Walnut Creek, CA: Left Coast Press, 2008). I am grateful to Lee Gutkind for this insight.

7.   Michael Seitzman, "Good Wins Over Evil. Period." Posted March 22,2010. http://www.huffingtonpost.com/michael-seitzman/good-wins-over-evil-perio_b_508491.html

8. Sam Youngman, "White House Unloads Anger Over Criticism from 'Professional Left.'" http://thehill.com/homenews/administration/113431-white-house-unloads-on-professional-left

9. See, for example, D. Soyini Madison, "Dangerous Ethnography," in Norman K. Denzin and Michael D. Giardina (eds.), *Qualitative Inquiry and Social Justice* (Walnut Creek, CA: Left Coast Press, 2009), 187–197. In that same volume, see also Ian Stronach, "Rethinking Words, Concepts, Stories, and Theories: Sensing a New World?" 248–278.

10. James Zogby, "Frightening GOP Behavior." http://www.huffingtonpost.com/james-zogby/frightening-gop-behavior_b_508969.html

11. Stephen Schlesinger, "The Party of Anger." http://www.huffingtonpost.com/stephen-schlesinger/the-party-of-anger_b_508252.html

12. Timothy Egan, "House of Anger." http://opinionator.blogs.nytimes.com/2010/03/24/house-of-anger/?hp

13. Much of the substance and language of this narrative is drawn from Sebastien Gorka and David Kilcullen, "Who's Winning the Battle for Narrative? Al-Qaida versus the United States and its Allies," *Influence Warfare* (New York: Praeger, 2009).

14. This thesis is elaborated in Jeffry Halverson, H. L. Goodall, Jr., and Steven R. Corman, *Master Narratives of Islamist Extremists* (New York: Palgrave Macmillan, 2010).

15. Andrea Elliott, "The Jihadi Next Door," *New York Times Magazine*, January 31, 2010. http://www.nytimes.com/2010/01/31/magazine/31Jihadist-t.htm

16. David Sunday, "Ted Olson: Same-Sex Marriage is a Conservative Value." http://videocafe.crooksandliars.com/node/38878

17. For one example, please see H. L. Goodall, Jr., and Seth Wiener, "Creating the right reality: Communication message strategies and the Republican party," *Cultural Studies—Critical Methodologies*, 8 (May 2008):135–158.

Chapter 2. Binary Opposites and Narrative IEDs

1. H. L. Goodall, Jr., *A Need to Know: The Clandestine History of a CIA Family* (Walnut Creek, CA: Left Coast Press, 2006).

2. Nica24, "We had eight years of Bush and Cheney, Now you get mad!?" Posted on Sunday, March 28, 2010 at 06:20:55 PM PDT. http://www.dailykos.com/storyonly/2010/3/28/851912/-We-had-eight-years-of-Bush-and-Cheney,-Now-you-get-mad!

3. "IED" is an acronym for "improvised explosive device."

4. Clancy Sigal, "US liberals have lost their thunder." http://www.guardian.co.uk/commentisfree/cifamerica/2010/feb/24/tea-party-protests-liberals

5. Frank Rich, "The Axis of the Obsessed and Deranged." http://www.nytimes.com/2010/02/28/opinion/28rich.html?emc=eta1

6. Daniel Bernardi and Scott Ruston, "The Triangle of Death: Strategic Communication, Counterinsurgency Ops, and the Rumor Mill," paper presented at "The Political and Social Uses of Rumors" conference, Singapore, February, 2010.

7. Jonathan Weisman, "Protests, Rhetoric Feed Jihadists' Fire," *Wall Street Journal*, August 23, 2010. http://online.wsj.com/article/SB10001424052748703589804575445841837725272.html?mod=WSJ_hpp_MIDDLETopStories

8. Frank Rich, "How Fox Betrayed Petraeus," *New York Times*, August 21, 2010. http://www.nytimes.com/2010/08/22/opinion/22rich.html?_r=2&src=me&ref=homepage

9. Kirsten Powers, "The GOP's Long, Hot, Racist Summer," *Daily Beast*, August 22, 2010. http://www.thedailybeast.com/blogs-and-stories/2010-08-22/republicans-long-hot-racist-summer

10. For further explication of the role of binary opposite in the current global war on terror, please see H. L. Goodall, Jr., "Blood, Shit, and Tears: The Terrorist as Abject Other," Managing and Legislating Workplace Abjection," originally prepared for the University of York "Seminar on Abjection and Alterity," sponsored by the Economic and Social Research Council of the UK, September 23, 2009. A newer version of that paper is available on my website http://hlgoodall.com/essays.html

11. For more about this interdisciplinary team charged with "identifying and countering extremist narratives" please see the CSC website at http://comops.org

12. The term "civil discourse" is not a cheap replacement for "polite discourse." There is room for legitimate anger, passion, and argument in a civil discourse. But, as my friend Mark Kilpack once expressed it, "Your right to swing your arm ends at my nose."

13. For more on this approach to communication, please see Steven R. Corman, H. L. Goodall, Jr., and Angela Trethewey (eds.), *Weapons of Mass Persuasion: Strategic Communication to Combat Violent Extremism* (New York: Peter Lang, 2008).

14. Frank E. X. Dance, *Human Communication Theory: Original Essays* (New York: Holt, Rhinehart, & Winston, 1967).

15. Jezebel, retrieved from http://jezebel.com/5498461/conservative-blogger-calls-for-obamas-assassination-on-twitter

16. Paul Krugman, "Fear Strikes Out," *New York Times*, March 22, 2010. http://www.nytimes.com/2010/03/22/opinion/22krugman.html?hp

17. Leonard S. Rubenstein And Stephen N. Xenakis, "Doctors Without Morals." http://www.nytimes.com/2010/03/01/opinion/01xenakis.html?ref=opinion

18. Michael H. Posner, "Torture Violates U.S. and International Law and Should Never Be Allowed," in Stuart Gottleib (ed.), *Debating Terrorism and Counterterrorism: Conflicting Perspectives on Causes, Contexts, and Responses* (Washington, D.C.: CG Press, 2009), 307–320.

19. "Fate of McCain Anti-Torture Amendment Now Rests With House-Senate Conference." http://www.humanrightsfirst.org/us_law/etn/mccain/index.asp

20. Alan Dershowitz, "There is a Need to Bring an Unfortunate Practice Within the Bounds of the Law," in Stuart Gottleib, ibid., 320–335.

21. Justine Sharrock, "Oath Keepers in an Age of Treason," Mother Jones available online: http://motherjones.com/politics/2010/03/oath-keepers

22. Frank Rich, "The Axis of the Obsessed and Deranged."

23. For list with comments see http://www.propagandacritic.com/; see also http://www.propagandacritic.com/articles/intro.ipa.html for a list of the books published by the Institute.

24. Peter Beinart, "The Tea Party's Phony Populism," *Huffington Post*, April 15, 2010. http://www.thedailybeast.com/blogs-and-stories/2010-04-15/the-tea-partys-fake-populism/#

25. J. K. Rowling, "The Nasty Party," *Daily Kos*, April 16, 2010. http://www.dailykos.com/storyonly/2010/4/16/857871/-J.K.-Rowling-on-conservatives:-the-nasty-party

26. J. Michael Waller, *Fighting the War of Ideas Like a Real War* (Washington, D.C.: The Institute of Politics Press, 2007). Please see chapter 5. The list of advantages is found on p. 109.

27. Kristin Fleischer, "Ridicule as Strategic Communication." http://comops.org/journal/2010/03/09/ridicule-as-strategic-communication/

28. For a summary of Burke's ideas, please see Kenneth Burke, *On Symbols and Society*. Edited, with an introduction, by J. Gusfield (Chicago: University of Chicago Press, 1989).

Chapter 3. Birthers, Social Justice & the Texas Textbook Massacre

1. Kenneth Burke, *On Symbols and Society*, ed. Joseph Gusfield (Chicago: University of Chicago Press, 1989).

2. Alasdair MacIntyre, *After Virtue: A Study in Moral Theory* (South Bend, IN: University of Notre Dame Press, 1984), 8.

3. Richard Hofstadter, "The Paranoid Style in American Politics," *Harper's Magazine*, November 1964, 77-86.

4. Hofstadter, 85.

5. Malcolm Gladwell, *The Tipping Point* (Philadelphia: Little, Brown, 2000).

6. For a comprehensive account of the Birthers movement and litigation, see http://en.wikipedia.org/wiki/Barack_Obama_citizenship_conspiracy_theories

7. Angie Drobnic Holan, "Obama used a Koran? No, he didn't." http://www.politifact.com/truth-o-meter/article/2007/dec/20/chain-email-gets-obama-religion-wrong/

8. Retrieved from http://www.snopes.com/politics/obama/muslim.asp

9. Quoted in Jake Sherman and Martin Kady, "Islam Group Ridicules Muslim 'Spies' Claim," *Politico.com* (October 14, 2009). http://www.politico.com/news/stories/1009/28283.html

10. For more on Fred Phelps and his beliefs, see his church website at: www.godhatesfags.com

11. Debra Burlingame and Thomas Joscelyn, "Gitmo's Indefensible Lawyers." http://online.wsj.com/article/SB10001424052748704131404575117611125872740.html. See also the Council on Foreign Relations comprehensive account of Sharia law, retrieved at: http://www.cfr.org/publication/8034/

12. "Ken Starr: Liz Cheney Wrong For Attacking Department Of Justice Attorneys (VIDEO)." http://www.huffingtonpost.com/2010/03/09/ken-starr-liz-cheney-wron_n_491182.html

13. Communication scholars Garth Jowett and Victoria O'Donnell define propaganda as "the deliberate, systematic attempt to shape perceptions, manipulate cognitions, and direct behavior to achieve a response that furthers the desired intent of the propagandist." *Propaganda and Persuasion.* 4th ed. (Thousand Oaks, CA: Sage Publications, 2006). For a good overview of the history of propaganda, see the Southwatch site at http://www.sourcewatch.org/index.php?title=Propaganda

14. For a good history of Bernays, see Stuart Ewen, *PR! A Social History of Spin* (New York: Basic Books, 1998).

15. See, for example, "Appendix I: PSYOP Techniques" from Psychological Operations Field Manual No.33-1 published by Headquarters; Department of the Army, in Washington, DC, on August 31, 1979.

16. See Jeffry Halverson, H. L. Goodall, Jr., and Steven R. Corman, *Master Narratives of Islamic Extremists* (New York: Palgrave Macmillan, 2010).

17. For a quick overview of the concept and its roots in various religious and faith traditions, see http://en.wikipedia.org/wiki/Social_justice. For a more detailed account, see John Rawls, *A theory of justice* (Cambridge, MA: Harvard University Press, 1971).

18. "Beck: Social justice 'is a perversion of the Gospel,' 'not what Jesus was saying'." http://mediamatters.org/mmtv/201003110017

19. Steve Benen, "Beck Doubles Down on Opposition to 'Social Justice'." http://www.washingtonmonthly.com/archives/individual/2010_03/022812.php

20. Hanna Siegel, "Christians Rip Glenn Beck Over 'Social Justice' Slam." http://abcnews.go.com/WN/glenn-beck-social-justice-christians-rage-back-nazism/story?id=10085008

21. Michael Bader, "We Need to Have Empathy for Tea Partiers." http://www.psychologytoday.com/node/39146

22. This insight and reference was "gifted" to me by communication scholar Jin Brown.

23. A thank you to Jin Brown, again.

24. "Rage Grows in America: AntiGovernment Conspiracies." http://www.adl.org/special_reports/rage-grows-in-America/mainstream-media.asp

25. James Poniewozik, "Glenn Beck: The Fears of a Clown." http://www.time.com/time/arts/article/0,8599,1890174,00.html

26. I'm not being pejorative here; he actually uses and promotes the term "extremist" on his website as a recruitment tool: http://www.glennbeck.com/

27. Bob Cesca, "Glenn Beck: the Televangelist Con Man Selling God's Plan for America," *Huffington Post*, April 21, 2010. http://www.huffingtonpost.com/bob-cesca/glenn-beck-the-televangel_b_546417.html

28. Michael Novak, "Defining Social Justice." http://www.firstthings.com/article/2007/01/defining-social-justice-29

29. Tony Judt, *Ill Fares the Land* (New York: Penguin Press, 2010).

30. "Texas Textbook MASSACRE: 'Ultraconservatives' Approve Radical Changes To State Education Curriculum." http://www.huffingtonpost.com/2010/03/13/texas-textbook-massacre-u_n_498003.html#s73775

31. Laurie Fendrich, "The Enlightenment, Texas Style." http://chronicle.com/blog-Post/The-Enlightenment-Texas-Style/21791/?sid=at&utm_source=at&utm_medium=en

32. James C. McKinley, Jr., "Texas Conservatives Win Curriculum Change." http://www.nytimes.com/2010/03/13/education/13texas.html?adxnnl=1&ref=general&src=me&adxnnlx=1268575372-ULEPHQBsDDJxL88L6G6KHA

33. For more about John Calvin: http://www.historylearningsite.co.uk/John_Calvin.htm

34. For a quick summary see: http://en.wikipedia.org/wiki/Strengths_and_weaknesses_of_evolution

35. Cited in Michael Ruse, "Philosophers Rip Darwin," *The Chronicle of Higher Education*, March 7, 2010, http://chronicle.com/article/What-Darwins-Doubters-Get/64457/

36. Retrieved at http://www.brainyquote.com/quotes/quotes/m/maferguson146000.html

37. Retrieved at http://www.snopes.com/politics/quotes/raskin.asp

38. Heather S. Gregg, "Fighting the Jihad of the Pen: Countering Revolutionary Islam's Ideology," *Terrorism and Political Violence*, 22 (April 2010): 292–314.

39. Lawrence Frey and Kevin Carragee, *Communication Activism* (Cresskill, NJ: Hampton Press, 2007).

40. Excerpted from Stephen John Hartnett, "Communication, Social Justice, and Joyful Commitment," *Western Journal of Communication*, 74 (January–February 2010): 68–93.

Chapter 4. Left at the War

1.   1. Michael Berube, *The Left at War* (New York: NYU Press, 2009), 151.

2.   Ronald Radosh, "How the Left Lost America," *New York Sun*, May 31, 2006. http://www.nysun.com/arts/how-the-left-lost-america/33568/

3.   Retrieved at http://www.ontheissues.org/2008/barack_obama_war_+_peace. htm

4.   H. L.Goodall, Jr., Angela Trethewey, and Steven R. Corman, "The Story Behind Obama's Cairo Speech." http://comops.org/journal/2009/06/05/ the-story-behind-obamas-cairo-speech/

5.   H. L.Goodall, Jr. "Obama's Nobel Speech Opens Narra- tive Possibilities." http://comops.org/journal/2009/12/14/ obamas-nobel-speech-opens-narrative-possibilities/

6.   H. L.Goodall, Jr., "The Afghanistan Narrative Gap and Its Consequences." http://comops.org/journal/2009/10/07/ the-afghanistan-narrative-gap-and-its-consequences/

7.   "Obama's Nobel Remarks," *New York Times*, December 10, 2009. http://www. nytimes.com/2009/12/11/world/europe/11prexy.text.html

8.   "Remarks by the President in Address to the Nation on the Way Forward in Afghanistan and Pakistan," White House press release, December 1, 2009. http://www.whitehouse.gov/the-press-office/ remarks-president-address-nation-way-forward-afghanistan-and-pakistan

9.   Kristi Keck, "U.S. must win Afghan hearts and minds, commander says." http://www.cnn.com/2009/POLITICS/09/28/afghanistan.obama/index.html

10. "Obama Blasts Defense Establishment." http://www.military.com/news/ article/August-2009/obama-blasts-defense-establishment-congress.html

11. Paul Berman, "Paul Berman's Response," *Dissent*, Spring 2007. http://www. dissentmagazine.org/article/?article=774

12. For a quick summary of the HTS, see http://en.wikipedia.org/wiki/Human_ Terrain_System; for the American Anthropological Association critique of

the project, see http://www.aaanet.org/issues/policy-advocacy/CEAUSSIC-Releases-Final-Report-on-Army-HTS-Program.cfm

13. U.S. Department of Defense, "First Minerva Research Initiative Awards Announced." http://www.defense.gov/releases/release.aspx?releaseid=12407

14. Please visit our CSC website: http://www.comops.org

15. Or "confuses" them, as my good friend and anti-war activist Stephen Hartnett once put it. Despite our disagreement over the war, he has co-authored a fine book that I highly recommend. See Stephen Hartnett and Laura Stengrim, *Globalization & Empire: The U.S. Invasion of Iraq, Free Markets, and The Twilight of Democracy* (Tuscaloosa: University of Alabama Press, 2006).

16. For an excellent overview of Qutb's thinking and influence, see Paul Berman, "The Philosopher of Islamic Terror," *New York Times Magazine*, March 23, 2003. http://www.nytimes.com/2003/03/23/magazine/23GURU.html

17. See, for example, David L. Altheide, *Terror Post 9/11 and the Media* (New York: Peter Lang, 2009).

18. See, for example, Andrea Elliott's account of a nice Alabama boy, nomme de guerre Abu Monsoor al-Amriki, who has risen to the leadership of al-Qaeda backed insurgency in Somalia ("The Jihadist Next Door," *New York Times Magazine*, January 31, 2010).

19. See his "FBI Most Wanted" poster here: http://www.fbi.gov/wanted/terrorists/gadahn_a.htm

20. Ethan Sacks, "U.S.-born Al Qaeda cleric Anwar Al-Awlaki calls for American Muslims to wage jihad against homeland." http://www.nydailynews.com/news/world/2010/03/18/2010-03-18_usborn_al_qaeda_cleric_anwar_alawlaki_calls_for_american_muslims_to_wage_jihad_a.html#ixzz0ijoeggoy

21. Retrieved at http://en.wikipedia.org/wiki/Adam_Yahiye_Gadahn

22. "Colleen LaRose: all-American neighbour or terrorist Jihad Jane?" http://www.guardian.co.uk/world/2010/mar/10/colleen-la-rose-jihad-jane-terrorism-arrest

23. Retrieve his "manifesto" at: Joe Weisenthal, "The Insane Manifesto Of Austin Texas Crash Pilot Joseph Andrew Stack." http://www.businessinsider.com/joseph-andrew-stacks-insane-manifesto-2010-2

24. David Damron, "Palin says 'reload,'" blog. http://blogs.orlandosentinel.com/news_politics/2010/03/palin-says-reload-puts-a-gun-sight-target-on-kosmas-this-fall.html

25. Southern Poverty Law Center, "Rage on the Right," March 2010. http://www.splcenter.org/get-informed/intelligence-report/browse-all-issues/2010/spring/rage-on-the-right

26. Lee Siegel, "The New Republican War Room." http://www.thedailybeast.com/blogs-and-stories/2010-03-27/the-new-republican-war-room/

27. John Avlon, "Militia Targets Democrats." http://www.thedailybeast.com/blogs-and-stories/2010-03-24/militia-targets-democrats/2/

28. Ibid.

29. Ibid.

30. Retrieved at http://sipseystreetirregulars.blogspot.com/

31. Visit their website at http://www.godhatesfags.com/

32. Tania Moxley, "Church planning anti-gay protests." http://www.roanoke.com/news/nrv/wb/241180

33. For a discussion of how digital tribes create a sense of shared community, please see Tyrone Adams and Stephen A. Smith (eds.), *Electronic Tribes: The Virtual Worlds of Geeks, Gamers, Shamans, and Scammers* (Austin: University of Texas Press, 2008).

34. Mona Gable, "Why Palin is not only an airhead but dangerous." http://www.huffingtonpost.com/mona-gable/why-sarah-palin-is-not-on_b_515428.html

35. Thanks to Pamela McWherter for this question: "Don't you find it ironic that they claim a literal interpretation of the Bible but not of their own words?"

36. A "jihobbyist" is someone who uses the Internet to troll extremist websites and who identifies with the al-Qaeda ideology, but who does not act on it. For an application of the difference between a jihadi and a jihobbyist, see Michael B. Farrell, "JihadJane case suggests rising threat from 'jihobbyists.'" http://www.csmonitor.com/USA/2010/0319/Jihad-Jane-case-suggests-rising-threat-from-online-jihobbyists

37. Elaine Walster, G. William Walster, and Ellen Bersheid, *Equity: Theory and Research* (Boston: Allyn & Bacon, 1978).

38. For details, see http://www.fcc.gov/telecom.html

39. As measured by the Pew Global Attitudes Project. For most recent poll showing the vast improvement under President Obama as well as the chart of world attitudes since 2000, see http://pewglobal.org/reports/display.php?ReportID=264

Chapter 5. The Academic Dilemma

1. For examples of that critique, see Janice Newson and Howard Buchbinder, *The University Means Business: Universities, Corporations and Academic Work* (Toronto: Garamond, 1988); Stanley Aronowitz, *The Knowledge Factory: Dismantling the Corporate University and Creating Higher Learning* (Boston: Beacon, 2000); Richard S. Ruch, "Higher Ed, Inc.," *The Rise the For Profit University* (Baltimore: John Hopkins University Press; 2001); Sheila Slaughter, *Academic Capitalism: Politics, Policies and the Entrepreneurial University* (Baltimore: John Hopkins University Press, 1999).

2. For an excellent example of this far-left argument, see Nick Dyer-Witheford, "Cognitive Capitalism and the Contested Campus," *European Journal of Higher Arts Education, Issue 2*, February 2005. http://firgoa.usc.es/drupal/node/27141

3. See Godfrey Hodgson, *The World Turned Right Side Up: A History of Conservative Ascendancy in America* (Boston: Houghton Mifflin, 1996), 75–77.

4. The Kaufman Foundation is an excellent leader and example of the entrepreneurial metaphor in higher education. See their website: http://www.kauffman.org/Section.aspx?id=About_The_Foundation

5. Figures for tuition and fees at the University of Pennsylvania are taken from their archival records. Retrieved at http://www.archives.upenn.edu/histy/features/tuition/1970.html. Figures for Shepherd are drawn from memory of my own cancelled checks and the current *Bulletin*.

6. For a comprehensive, fifty-state summary of state support for higher education since 1960, see http://www.grapevine.ilstu.edu/

7. See http://asunews.asu.edu/20100303_budgetfacts

8. "Bill Maher Blasts Tea Party for Ignoring Defense Spending," *Huffington Post*, April 24, 2010. http://www.huffingtonpost.com/2010/04/24/bill-maher-to-tea-baggers_n_550430.html

9. Marc Ambinder, "Have Conservatives Gone Mad?" *The Atlantic*, April 23, 2010. http://www.theatlantic.com/politics/archive/2010/04/have-conservatives-gone-mad/39417/

10. "Bill Maher Blasts Tea Party for Ignoring Defense Spending."

11. Marc Ambinder, "Have Conservatives Gone Mad?"

12. Karl Rove, *Courage And Consequence: My Life as a Conservative in the Fight* (New York: Threshold Editions, 2010), 520.

13. Bruce Speck, "The Growing Role of Private Giving in Financing the Modern University," *New Directions for Higher Education*, 149 (March 2010): 7–16.

14. Harry Torrance, "Research Quality and Research Governance in the United Kingdom: From Methodology to Management," in Norman K. Denzin and Michael D. Giardina (eds.), *Qualitative Inquiry and the Conservative Challenge* (Walnut Creek, CA: Left Coast Press, 2006), 127–148.

15. Julianne Cheek, "The Challenge of Tailor-Made Research Quality: The RQF in Australia," in Norman K. Denzin and Michael D. Giardina (eds.), *Qualitative Inquiry and the Conservative Challenge* (Walnut Creek, CA: Left Coast Press, 2006), 109–126.

16. Norman K. Denzin and Michael D. Giardina, "Introduction," in Norman K. Denzin and Michael D. Giardina (eds.), *Qualitative Inquiry and the Conservative Challenge* (Walnut Creek, CA: Left Coast Press, 2006), ix–x.

17.   Ibid., xx.

18.   Robert F. Kennedy, *Crimes Against Nature: How George W. Bush and His Corporate Pals are Plundering the Country and Hijacking Our Democracy* (New York: HarperCollins, 2004); see also Chris Mooney, *The Republican War on Science* (New York: Basic Books, 2005).

19.   In fact, our private and public universities rank at the very top of all universities in the world, see http://www.topuniversities.com/university-rankings/world-university-rankings/2009/results. And while it is true that K-12 education continues to suffer an inexcusable 70 percent high school graduation rate—the lowest in the developed world—the reasons for this "failure" have everything to do with a variety of sociological and political factors, from the rise of single-parent households to reduced funding for inner city schools, a lack of motivation to complete school, and a lack of special programs designed to assist the needy. Neither "No Child Left Behind" nor "Race to the Top" seriously addresses those problems.

20.   The root cause is "failing students, not failing schools": for a brief overview, see Jim Taylor, "Failing Students, Not Failing Schools." http://www.huffingtonpost.com/dr-jim-taylor/failing-students-not-fail_b_534797.html

21.   David R. Jones, "Education Reform: America's Third Rail," *Huffington Post,* March 11, 2010. http://www.huffingtonpost.com/david-jones/education-reform-americas_b_495030.html

22.   Jeffry Halverson, H. L. Goodall, Jr., and Steven R. Corman, *Master Narratives of Islamist Extremists* (New York: Palgrave Macmillan, 2010).

Chapter 6. Learning from Obama and Learning from our Enemies

1.   Joe Cirincioni, "The Start of a New Obama Narrative." http://www.huffingtonpost.com/joe-cirincione/the-start-of-a-new-obama_b_515305.html

2.   Peter Beinard, "Obama's Power Surge," *Daily Beast,* March 28, 2010. http://www.thedailybeast.com/blogs-and-stories/2010-03-28/obamas-power-grab/?cid=hp:mainpromo2

3.   Eric Alterman, "Obama Betrays the Left Again," *The Daily Beast,* April 3, 2010, http://www.thedailybeast.com/blogs-and-stories/2010-03-31/obamas-oil-betrayal/?cid=hp:mostpopular1

4.   Madison Gray, "Sarah Palin's Facebook Oil Spill Rant," Time Newsfeed. http://newsfeed.time.com/2010/06/04/sarah-palins-facebook-blasts-environmentalists-for-oil-spill/#ixzz0w1vSmwGQ

5.   Dan Gilgoff, "Christians from political left and right sign 'Civility Covenant.'" http://www.cnn.com/2010/POLITICS/03/26/christian.civility.covenant/index.html?eref=rss_latest&utm_source=feedburner&utm_medium=feed&utm_campaign=Feed:%20rss/cnn_latest%20%28RSS:%20Most%20Recent%29

6.   Carol Howard Merritt, "Why Evangelicalism Is Failing A New Generation," *Huffington Post*, April 1, 2010. http://www.huffingtonpost.com/carol-howard-merritt/why-evangelicalism-is-fai_b_503971.html

7.   Frank Schaeffer, "The Evangelical 'Mainstream' Insanity Behind the Michigan 'End Times' Militia," *Huffington Post*, April 2, 2010. http://www.huffingtonpost.com/frank-schaeffer/the-evangelical-mainstrea_b_520990.html

8.   Eileen Sullivan and Devlin Barrett, "FBI Investigating Extremist Group Letters Telling Governors to Leave Office," *Huffington Post*, April 2, 2010. http://www.huffingtonpost.com/2010/04/02/fbi-investigating-extremi_n_522984.html

9.   Mike Signer, "How to beat the demagogues," *Daily Beast*, March 27 2010. http://www.thedailybeast.com/blogs-and-stories/2010-03-27/how-to-beat-the-demagogues/?cid=hp:beastoriginalsL2

10. Tom Halsted, "What's Happening to America," *Huffington Post*, March 28, 2010. http://www.huffingtonpost.com/tom-halsted/whats-happening-to-americ_b_515181.html

11. Thomas H. Johnson, "The Taliban Insurgency and an Analysis of *Shabnamah* (Night Letters)," *Small Wars and Insurgencies*, 18, (September 2007): 317–344.

12. Caroline Myss, "Are Republican Right-Wingers Homeland Security Threats?" *Huffington Post*, March 29, 2010. http://www.huffingtonpost.com/caroline-myss/are-republican-right-wing_b_516467.html

13. Nick Bunkley and Charlie Savage, "Militia Charged With Plotting to Murder Officers," *New York Times*, March 29, 2010. http://www.nytimes.com/2010/03/30/us/30militia.html?hp

14. YouTube video retrieved at http://www.dailykos.com/story/2010/3/29/852032/-Breaking-Militia-raids-were-over-plot-to-levy-war-against-the-US-Government

15. "Distrust, Discontent, Anger and Partisan Rancor: The People and Their Government," The Pew Research Center for People and the Press, April 18, 2010. http://people-press.org/report/606/trust-in-government

16. Personal communication via email, April 19, 2010.

17. George Lakoff, "The Poll Democrats Need to Know About," *Huffington Post*, April 15, 2010. http://www.huffingtonpost.com/george-lakoff/the-poll-democrats-need-t_b_537993.html

18. Roy F. Baumeister , Ellen Bratslavsky, Catrin Finkenauer, and Kathleen D. Vohs, "Bad is stronger than good," *Review of General Psychology*, 5, (4): 323–370.

19. Kenneth Burke, *A Rhetoric of Motives* (Berkeley: University of California Press, 1969).

20. Ernest Bormann, *The Force of Fantasy: Restoring the American Dream* (Carbondale: Southern Illinois University Press, 1985).

21. "Obama's November 7, 2007, speech on the 'American Dream,'" CNN Politics.com. http://www.cnn.com/2007/POLITICS/12/21/obama.trans.americandream/

Chapter 7. The Core Counter-Narrative

1. Froukje Demant and Beatrice De Graaf , "How to Counter Racial Narratives: Dutch Deradicalization Policy in the Case of Moluccan and Islamic Radicals," *Studies in Conflict & Terrorism*, 33, (April, 2010): 408–428.

References

Adams, Tyrone, and Stephen A. Smith, eds. *Electronic Tribes: The Virtual Worlds of Geeks, Gamers, Shamans, and Scammers*. Austin: University of Texas Press, 2008.

Alterman, Eric. "Obama Betrays the Left Again." *Daily Beast*, April 3, 2010. http://www.thedailybeast.com/blogs-and-stories/2010-03-31/obamas-oil-betrayal/?cid=hp:mostpopular1.

Altheide, David L. *Terror Post 9/11 and the Media*. New York: Peter Lang, 2009.

Ambinder, Marc. "Have Conservatives Gone Mad?" *The Atlantic*, April 23, 2010. http://www.theatlantic.com/politics/archive/2010/04/have-conservatives-gone-mad/39417/.

Aronowitz, Stanley. *The Knowledge Factory: Dismantling the Corporate University and Creating Higher Learning*. Boston: Beacon, 2000.

Avlon, John. "Scary New GOP Poll: Wingnuts Hijacking Politics." http://www.thedailybeast.com/blogs-and-stories/2010-03-22/scary-new-gop-poll/?cid=hp:exc.

Bailyn, Bernard. *The Ideological Origins of the American Revolution*. Cambridge, MA: Belknap/Harvard University Press, 1992.

Baumeister, Roy F., Ellen Bratslavsky, Catrin Finkenauer, and Kathleen D. Vohs. "Bad is stronger than good." *Review of General Psychology*, 5, 4 (2001): 323–370.

Beinard, Peter. "Obama's Power Surge." *Daily Beast*, March 28, 2010. http://www.thedailybeast.com/blogs-and-stories/2010-03-28/obamas-power-grab/?cid=hp:mainpromo2.

Beinart, Peter. "The Tea Party's Phony Populism." *Huffington Post*, April 15, 2010. http://www.thedailybeast.com/blogs-and-stories/2010-04-15/the-tea-partys-fake-populism/#.

Berman, Paul. "The Philosopher of Islamic Terror." *New York Times Magazine*, March 23, 2003. http://www.nytimes.com/2003/03/23/magazine/23GURU.html

———. "Paul Berman's Response." *Dissent*, Spring 2007. http://www.dissentmagazine.org/article/?article=774.

Bernardi, Daniel, and Scott Ruston. "The Triangle of Death: Strategic Communication, Counterinsurgency Ops, and the Rumor Mill." Paper presented at "The Political and Social Uses of Rumors" conference, Singapore, February, 2010.

Berube, Michael. *The Left at War*. New York: NYU Press, 2009.

"Bill Maher Blasts Tea Party for Ignoring Defense Spending." *Huffington Post*, April 24, 2010. http://www.huffingtonpost.com/2010/04/24/bill-maher-to-tea-baggers_n_550430.html.

Boehlert, Eric. "Post-Hutaree: How Glenn Beck and Fox News Spread The Militia Message." *Huffington Post*, April 6, 2010. http://www.huffingtonpost.com/eric-boehlert/post-hutaree-how-glenn-be_b_526687.html.

Brachman, Jarret. "Jihad Straight to Your Ipod? AQAP's Latest Gimmick." HTTP: JARRETBRACHMAN, April 20, 2010. http://jarretbrachman.net/?p=646.

Burke, Kenneth. *On Symbols and Society*. Ed. Joseph Gusfield. Chicago: University of Chicago Press, 1989.

Cable News Rating April 2010. *Huffington Post*, April 27, 2010. http://www.huffingtonpost.com/2010/04/28/cable-news-ratings-april_n_554295.html.

Cesca, Bob. "Glenn Beck: the Televangelist Con Man Selling God's Plan for America." *Huffington Post*, April 21, 2010. http://www.huffingtonpost.com/bob-cesca/glenn-beck-the-televangel_b_546417.html.

Cheek, Julianne. "The Challenge of Tailor-Made Research Quality: The RQF in Australia." In Norman K. Denzin and Michael D. Giardina, eds.,

109–126. *Qualitative Inquiry and the Conservative Challenge.* Walnut Creek, CA: Left Coast Press, 2006.

Cheong, Pauline Hope. "A Broader View of Internet Radicalization." *COMOPS – A Journal of Strategic Communication,* March 2009. http://comops.org/journal/2009/03/26/a-broader-view-of-internet-radicalization/.

Cirincioni, Joe. "The Start of a New Obama Narrative." http://www.huffingtonpost.com/joe-cirincione/the-start-of-a-new-obama_b_515305.html.

Cohen, Patricia. "'Epistemic Closure'? Those Are Fighting Words." *New York Times Book Review,* April 27, 2010. http://www.nytimes.com/2010/04/28/books/28conserv.html?ref=books.

Corman, Steven R., H. L. Goodall, Jr., and Angela Trethewey, eds. *Weapons of Mass Persuasion: Strategic Communication to Combat Violent Extremism.* New York: Peter Lang, 2008.

Dance, Frank E. X. *Human Communication Theory: Original Essays.* New York: Holt, Rhinehart & Winston, 1967.

Demant, Froukje, and Beatrice De Graaf. "How to Counter Racial Narratives: Dutch Deradicalization Policy in the Case of Moluccan and Islamic Radicals." *Studies in Conflict & Terrorism, 33,* (April, 2010): 408–428.

Denzin, Norman K., and Michael D. Giardina. "Introduction: Qualitative Inquiry and the Conservative Challenge." In Norman K. Denzin and Michael D. Giardina, eds., ix–x. *Qualitative Inquiry and the Conservative Challenge.* Walnut Creek, CA: Left Coast Press, 2006.

Denzin, Norman K., and Michael D. Giardina, eds. *Qualitative Inquiry and Social Justice.* Walnut Creek, CA: Left Coast Press, 2009.

Dershowitz, Alan. "There is a Need to Bring an Unfortunate Practice Within the Bounds of the Law." In Stuart Gottleib, ed., 320–335. *Debating Terrorism and Counterterrorism: Conflicting Perspectives on Causes, Contexts, and Responses.* Washington, D.C.: CG Press, 2009.

Dyer-Witheford, Nick. "Cognitive Capitalism and the Contested Campus." *European Journal of Higher Arts Education, Issue 2,* February 2005. http://firgoa.usc.es/drupal/node/27141.

Egan, Timothy. "The Desert Derangement Syndrome." *New York Times,* April 28, 2010. http://opinionator.blogs.nytimes.com/2010/04/28/desert-derangement-syndrome/?ref=opinion.

Egan, Timothy. "House of Anger." http://opinionator.blogs.nytimes.com /2010/03/24/house-of-anger/?hp.

Elliott, Andrea. "The Jihadist Next Door," *New York Times Magazine,* January 31, 2010. http://www.nytimes.com/2010/01/31/magazine/31Jihadist-t. htm.

Ewen, Stuart. *PR! A Social History of Spin.* New York: Basic Books, 1998.

"FBI Investigating Extremist Group Letters Telling Governors to Leave Office." *Huffington Post,* April 2, 2010. http://www.huffingtonpost. com/2010/04/02/fbi-investigating-extremi_n_522984.html.

Fisher, W. R. *Human communication as narration: Toward a philosophy of reason, value, and action.* Columbia: University of South Carolina Press, 1987.

Fleischer, Kristin. "Ridicule as Strategic Communication." http://comops. org/journal/2010/03/09/ridicule-as-strategic-communication/.

Frey, Lawrence, and Kevin Carragee. *Communication Activism.* Cresskill, NJ: Hampton Press, 2007.

Gable, Mona. "Why Palin is not only an airhead but dangerous." http:// www.huffingtonpost.com/mona-gable/why-sarah-palin-is-not-on_b_515428.html.

Ginsberg, Allen. "America." http://www.writing.upenn.edu/~afilreis/88/ america.html.

Gladwell, Malcolm. *The Tipping Point.* Philadelphia: Little, Brown, 2000.

Goodall, Jr., H. L. "Bud". "The Afghanistan Narrative Gap and Its Consequences." http://comops.org/journal/2009/10/07/ the-afghanistan-narrative-gap-and-its-consequences/.

———. *A Need to Know: The Clandestine History of a CIA Family.* Walnut Creek, CA: Left Coast Press, 2006.

———. "Blood, Shit, and Tears: The Terrorist as Abject Other," Managing and Legislating Workplace Abjection," University of York "Seminar on Abjection and Alterity," sponsored by the Economic and Social Research Council of the UK, September 23, 2009. A newer version of that paper is available at http://hlgoodall.com/essays.html.

———, and Seth Wiener (2008). "Creating the right reality: Communication message strategies and the Republican party." *Cultural Studies—Critical Methodologies,* 8 (May 2008): 135–158.

————. "Obama's Nobel Speech Opens Narrative Possibilities." http://comops.org/journal/2009/12/14/obamas-nobel-speech-opens-narrative-possibilities/.

————, Angela Trethewey, and Steven R. Corman. "The Story Behind Obama's Cairo Speech." http://comops.org/journal/2009/06/05/the-story-behind-obamas-cairo-speech/.

————. *Writing Qualitative Inquiry: Self, Stories, and Academic Life.* Walnut Creek, CA: Left Coast Press, 2008.

Gorka, Sebastien, and David Kilcullen. "Who's Winning the Battle for Narrative? Al-Qaida versus the United States and its Allies." *Influence Warfare.* New York: Praeger, 2009.

Gregg, Heather S. "Fighting the Jihad of the Pen: Countering Revolutionary Islam's Ideology." *Terrorism and Political Violence*, 22 (April 2010): 292–314.

Halsted, Tom. "What's Happening to America." *Huffington Post*, March 28, 2010. http://www.huffingtonpost.com/tom-halsted/whats-happening-to-americ_b_515181.html.

Halverson, Jeffry, H. L. Goodall, Jr., and Steven R. Corman. *Master Narratives of Islamist Extremists.* New York: Palgrave Macmillan, 2010.

Hartnett, Stephen John. "Communication, Social Justice, and Joyful Commitment." *Western Journal of Communication*, 74 (January-February 2010): 68–93.

Hartnett, Stephen, and Laura Stengrim. *Globalization & Empire: The U.S. Invasion of Iraq, Free Markets, and The Twilight of Democracy.* Tuscaloosa: University of Alabama Press, 2006.

Hodgson, Godfrey. *The World Turned Right Side Up: A History of Conservative Ascendancy in America.* Boston: Houghton Mifflin, 1996.

Hofstadter, Richard. "The Paranoid Style in American Politics." *Harper's Magazine*, November 1964:77–86.

"JihadJane case suggests rising threat from 'jihobbyists.'" http://www.csmonitor.com/USA/2010/0319/Jihad-Jane-case-suggests-rising-threat-from-online-jihobbyists.

Johnson, Thomas H. "The Taliban Insurgency and an Analysis of *Shabnamah* (Night Letters)." *Small Wars and Insurgencies, 18*, (September 2007):317–344.

Jones, David R. "Education Reform: America's Third Rail." *Huffington Post*, March 11, 2010. http://www.huffingtonpost.com/david-jones/education-reform-americas_b_495030.html.

Jowett, Garth, and Victoria O'Donnell. *Propaganda and Persuasion*. 4th ed. Thousand Oaks, CA: Sage Publications, 2006.

Judt, Tony. *Il Fares the Land*. New York: Penguin Press, 2010.

Kennedy, Robert F. *Crimes Against Nature: How George W. Bush and His Corporate Pals are Plundering the Country and Hijacking Our Democracy*. New York: HarperCollins, 2004.

Krugman, Paul. "Fear Strikes Out." *New York Times*, March 22, 2010. http://www.nytimes.com/2010/03/22/opinion/22krugman.html?hp.

Lakoff, George. *Don't Think of an Elephant: Know Your Values and Frame the Debate*. White River Junction, VT: Chelsea Green Publishing Company, 2004.

———. "The Obama Code." *Daily Kos*, February 24, 2009. http://www.dailykos.com/story/2009/2/24/04124/0642/643/701081.

———. "The Poll Democrats Need to Know About." *Huffington Post*, April 15, 2010. http://www.huffingtonpost.com/george-lakoff/the-poll-democrats-need-t_b_537993.html.

MacIntyre, Alasdair. *After Virtue: A Study in Moral Theory*. South Bend, IN: University of Notre Dame Press, 1984.

Merritt, Carol Howard. "Why Evangelicalism Is Failing A New Generation." *Huffington Post*, April 1, 2010. http://www.huffingtonpost.com/carol-howard-merritt/why-evangelicalism-is-fai_b_503971.html.

"Militia Charged With Plotting to Murder Officers." http://www.nytimes.com/2010/03/30/us/30militia.html?hp.

Mooney, Chris. *The Republican War on Science*. New York: Basic Books, 2005.

Myss, Caroline, "Are Republican Right-Wingers Homeland Security Threats?" *Huffington Post*, March 29, 2010. http://www.huffingtonpost.com/caroline-myss/are-republican-right-wing_b_516467.html.

"New GOP Poll: Wingnuts Hijacking Politics." http://www.thedailybeast.com/blogs-and-stories/2010-03-22/scary-new-gop-poll/?cid=hp:exc.

Newson, Janice, and Howard Buchbinder. *The University Means Business: Universities, Corporations and Academic Work*. Toronto: Garamond, 1988.

Nica24, "We had eight years of Bush and Cheney, Now you get mad!?" Posted on Sunday, March 28, 2010, at 06:20:55 PM PDT. http://www. dailykos.com/storyonly/2010/3/28/851912/-We-had-eight-years -of-Bush-and-Cheney,-Now-you-get-mad!

"Obama's Nobel Remarks." *New York Times*, December 10, 2009. http:// www.nytimes.com/2009/12/11/world/europe/11prexy.text.html.

"Obama's November 7, 2007, speech on the 'American Dream,'" CNN Politics.com. http://www.cnn.com/2007/POLITICS/12/21/obama.trans. americandream/.

Office of the Press Secretary, The White House. http://www.whitehouse. gov/the_press_office/RemarksbyPresidentBarackObamaOnChildren-sHealthInsuranceProgramBillSigning/.

———. http://www.whitehouse.gov/the-press-office/remarks-president-address-nation-way-forward-afghanistan-and-pakistan.

The Pew Research Center for People and the Press. "Distrust, Discontent, Anger and Partisan Rancor: The People and Their Government." April 18, 2010. http://people-press.org/report/606/trust-in-government.

Poniewozik, James. "Glenn Beck: The Fears of a Clown." http://www.time. com/time/arts/article/0,8599,1890174,00.html.

Posner, Michael H. "Torture Violates U.S. and International Law and Should Never Be Allowed." In Stuart Gottlieb, ed., 307–320. *Debating Terror-ism and Counterterrorism: Conflicting Perspectives on Causes, Contexts, and Responses*. Washington, D.C.: CG Press, 2009.

Powers, Kirsten. "The GOP's Long, Hot, Racist Summer." Daily Beast, August 22, 2010. http://www.thedailybeast.com/blogs-and-stories/2010-08-22/ republicans-long-hot-racist-summer.

Psychological Operations Field Manual No.33-1. Published by Headquar-ters; Department of the Army, Washington, D.C., on August 13, 1979.

Radosh, Ronald. "How the Left Lost America." *NY Sun*, May 31, 2006. http:// www.nysun.com/arts/how-the-left-lost-america/33568/.

Rawls, John. *A theory of justice*. Cambridge, MA: Harvard University Press, 1971.

Rich, Frank. "The Axis of the Obsessed and Deranged." http://www. nytimes.com/2010/02/28/opinion/28rich.html.

Rowling, J.K. "The Nasty Party." *Daily Kos*, April 16, 2010. http://www. dailykos.com/storyonly/2010/4/16/857871/-J.K.-Rowling-on-conservatives:-the-nasty-party.

Rove, Karl. *Courage And Consequence: My Life as a Conservative in the Fight*. New York: Threshold Editions, 2010.

Rubenstein, Leonard S., and Stephen N. Xenakis. "Doctors Without Morals." http://www.nytimes.com/2010/03/01/opinion/01xenakis. html?ref=opinion.

Ruch, Richard S. *Higher Ed, Inc: The Rise the For Profit University*. Baltimore, MD: John Hopkins University Press, 2001.

Ruse, Michael. "Philosophers Rip Darwin." *The Chronicle of Higher Education*, March 7, 2010. http://chronicle.com/article/What-Darwins-Doubters-Get/64457/.

Schaeffer, Frank. "The Evangelical 'Mainstream' Insanity Behind the Michigan 'End Times' Militia." *Huffington Post*, April 2, 2010. http://www.huffingtonpost.com/frank-schaeffer/the-evangelical-mainstrea_b_520990.html.

Schlesinger, Stephen. "The Party of Anger." http://www.huffingtonpost. com/stephen-schlesinger/the-party-of-anger_b_508252.html.

Scott, Robert L., and Donald K. Smith. "The Rhetoric of Confrontation." *The Quarterly Journal of Speech*, 60, 1 (November 1969): 1–8.

Seitzman, Michael. "Good Wins Over Evil. Period." Posted March 22, 2010. http://www.huffingtonpost.com/michael-seitzman/good-wins-over-evil-perio_b_508491.html.

Sharrock, Justine. "Oath Keepers in an Age of Treason." http://motherjones. com/politics/2010/03/oath-keepers.

Shea, Danny. "Cable News Rating April 2010." *Huffington Post*, April 27, 2010. http://www.huffingtonpost.com/2010/04/28/cable-news-ratings-april_n_554295.html.

Sherman, Jake, and Martin Kady. "Islam Group Ridicules Muslim 'Spies' Claim." *Politico.com* (October 14, 2009). http://www.politico.com/ news/stories/1009/28283.html.

Siegel, Lee. "The New Republican War Room." http://www.thedailybeast. com/blogs-and-stories/2010-03-27/the-new-republican-war-room/.

Signer, Mike. "How to beat the demagogues." *Daily Beast,* March 27 2010. http://www.thedailybeast.com/blogs-and-stories/2010-03-27/ how-to-beat-the-demagogues/?cid=hp:beastoriginalsL2.

Slaughter, Sheila. *Academic Capitalism: Politics, Policies and the Entrepreneurial University.* Baltimore, MD: John Hopkins University Press, 1999.

Southern Poverty Law Center. "Rage on the Right." http://www.splcenter. org/get-informed/intelligence-report/browse-all-issues/2010/spring/ rage-on-the-right.

Speck, Bruce. "The Growing Role of Private Giving in Financing the Modern University." *New Directions for Higher Education,* 149 (March 2010): 7–16.

Torrance, Harry. "Research Quality and Research Governance in the United Kingdom: From Methodology to Management." In Norman K. Denzin and Michael D. Giardina, eds., 127–148. *Qualitative Inquiry and the Conservative Challenge.* Walnut Creek, CA: Left Coast Press, 2006.

Trethewey, Angela, Steven R. Corman, and Bud Goodall. "Out of Their Heads and Into the Conversation: Countering Extremist Ideology." A COMOPS WHITE PAPER, September 14, 2009. http://comops.org/.

Waller, J. Michael. *Fighting the War of Ideas Like a Real War.* Washington, D.C.: The Institute of Politics Press, 2007.

Walster, Elaine, G. William Walster, and Ellen Bersheid. *Equity: Theory and Research.* Boston: Allyn & Bacon, 1978.

Weisman, Jonathan. "Protests, Rhetoric Feed Jihadists' Fire." *Wall Street Journal,* August 23, 2010. http://online.wsj.com/article/ SB10001424052748703589804575445841837725272. html?mod=WSJ_hpp_MIDDLETopStories.

Zogby, James. "Frightening GOP Behavior." http://www.huffingtonpost. com/james-zogby/frightening-gop-behavior_b_508969.html.

Index

About the Author

H. L. (Bud) Goodall, Jr., is Professor of Communication and former Director of the Hugh Downs School of Human Communication at Arizona State University. He is a senior fellow at the Consortium for Strategic Communication and an affiliated faculty member at the Center for the Study of Religion and Conflict. He is the author or co-author of twenty books and over one hundred articles, chapters, and papers. His edited volume, with Steve Corman and Angela Trethewey, *Weapons of Mass Persuasion: Strategic Communication and the War of Ideas*, is currently required reading for members of the defense and intelligence communities. A pioneer in the field of narrative ethnography he has studied high technology organizations, rock and roll bands, alternative forms of religion and spirituality in the southern United States, and recast his own life story in *A Need to Know: The Clandestine History of a CIA Family* (2006). With Eric Eisenberg and Angela Trethewey, he is the co-author of the award-winning textbook, *Organizational Communication: Balancing Creativity and Constraint*, now in its sixth edition, and he authored the highly acclaimed *Writing the New Ethnography* and *Writing Qualitative Inquiry*. His most recent work is in applying theories of communication and narratives to the challenge of countering ideological support for terrorism.